★ SCHOLASTIC

★

READ–ALOUD PLAYS

World War II

by Alexandra Hanson-Harding

New York • Toronto • London • Auckland • Sydney
Mexico City • New Delhi • Hong Kong • Buenos Aires

Teaching *Resources*

For Brian, Moses, and Jacob.

Cover design by Norma Ortiz
Cover illustration by Harry K. Whitver
Interior design by Melinda Belter
Interior illustrations by Mona Mark

ISBN 0-439-51895-4

Printed in the U.S.A.

1 2 3 4 5 6 7 8 9 10   40   11 10 09 08 07 06 05 04

Contents

Introduction

IMAGINE LIVING IN LONDON DURING THE BLITZ, being trapped behind barbed wire in an internment camp, or facing heavy fire as a soldier during D-Day. That's what students will be able to imagine as they act out these experiences in *Read-Aloud Plays: World War II.*

World War II was the pivotal event of the twentieth century. No war before or since killed so many or destroyed so much. Cities that had stood for a thousand years were left in smoldering ruins. Millions of innocent people were murdered and many families were shattered. The impact of that war still shapes the world we live in today.

This book of plays highlights five crucial moments in World War II. These plays will help students increase their understanding and awareness of this major historical period in a hands-on, active way. It can help to bring a story to life by immersing students in the dramas the characters face.

This book can be used in a number of different ways. You can have students read the various plays as an introduction to your teaching of World War II. Or, you can have students read the plays after they have spent time studying the war. You can do a simple in-class reading, or you can have students create an elaborate production with props and costumes, to perform for other classes. You can use just one or two of these plays, or have students perform all of them in order to gain a sense of the sweep of World War II.

This book can be used as part of the social studies curriculum, but it will help students develop language arts skills in reading, writing, and oral presentation as well. Each play is followed by a teacher's guide, which provides background material, thinking questions, and hands-on classroom activities to help extend the lessons in the text. Here are some suggestions to help you get even more out of this book:

1. Before students read a play, ask them what they know about the events the play covers. After reading the play, share the background information with students. Then, ask them what they learned, and how that differed from what they'd previously thought. Also ask them if the background information changed their perception of what happened during the play.

2. If you have time, encourage students to do more research on one of these events. Then they can work in teams to create posters, speeches, or other kinds of presentations to share with the class.

3. Or, alternatively, students can do research on other events that took place during the war, such as the Battle of Midway, the invasion of Italy, or the dropping of the atomic bomb. Then, using the plays in this book as models, they can create skits about these other wartime events. The possibilities are endless!

4. Ask students to place these events in time. Which of them overlap? Which happened over a short period of time? Which events led to other events in the book of plays (for example, how did the attack on Pearl Harbor lead to Manzanar? Was it the inevitable result of the attack? How might history have gone differently if certain events didn't happen?).

5. Have students examine the claims and circumstances of various characters in the play. They can write letters or speeches from the points of view of different characters and historical figures.

> **TIP:** Remember to give each student a chance to take part over the course of reading the plays. You might want to preread the plays and underline the largest parts so that everyone can get a fair shake. Also, some plays, especially those set during battles, have far more male characters than females. Out of fairness, give boys and girls a chance to try roles of the opposite gender.

I hope you will find these plays an engaging and entertaining way for students to learn more about World War II.

Sincerely,

Alexandra Hanson-Harding

RESOURCES: These plays were created with the help of many excellent newspaper and magazine articles, books, and Web sites. The following books were particularly helpful resources. You and your students may want to check them out for a more in-depth exploration of World War II.

Voyage of the Damned by Gordon Thomas and Max Morgan Witts
     (Stein and Day, 1974)
Children of the Blitz: Memories of Wartime Childhood compiled
     by Robert Westall (Viking Penguin Inc, 1985)
December 7, 1941: The Day the Japanese Attacked Pearl Harbor
     by Gordon William Prange (McGraw-Hill, 1988)
Farewell to Manzanar by Jeanne Wakatsuki Houston and James
     D. Houston (Houghton Mifflin, 1973)
D-Day: June 6, 1944 by Stephen Ambrose (Simon & Schuster, 1994)

Aboard the St. Louis

CHARACTERS

CLAUS-GOTTFRIED HOLTHUSEN, *director of the Hamburg-America Cruise Line*

GUSTAV SCHROEDER, *captain of the* St. Louis

MRS. BABETTE SPANIER, *passenger* • DR. FRITZ SPANIER, *passenger*

LUIS CLASING, *Hamburg-America Cruise Line agent in Havana*

MANUEL BENITEZ, *Cuba's director of immigration*

DR. JUAN REMOS, *Cuba's secretary of state* • RENATTA ABER, *age 7, passenger*

EVELYNE ABER, *age 5, passenger* • KLAUS OSTERMEYER, *first officer of the* St. Louis

HERBERT MANASSE, *member of the passenger committee*

MR. MAX LOEWE, *passenger* • MRS. ELISE LOEWE, *passenger*

OSKAR BLECHNER, *passenger* • BRANDLA FLAMBERG, *passenger*

FREDERICO BRU, *President of Cuba*

LAWRENCE BERENSON, *American lawyer*

JOSEPH C. HYMAN, *executive director of the American Jewish Joint Distribution Committee in New York*

FERDINAND MUELLER, *purser of the* St. Louis

MR. AARON POZNER, *passenger* • LEO JOCKL, *steward of the* St. Louis

JOSEF JOSEPH, *head of the passenger committee* • NARRATORS 1–3

SCENE 1

NARRATOR 1: May 3, 1939, Captain Gustav Schroeder meets with Claus-Gottfried Holthusen, director of the Hamburg-America Cruise Line at its Hamburg, Germany, headquarters.

CLAUS-GOTTFRIED HOLTHUSEN: This will be a special voyage. It will carry more than 900 refugees from Germany to Cuba.

GUSTAV SCHROEDER: Who are these refugees?

CLAUS-GOTTFRIED HOLTHUSEN: Just some Jews who want to leave Germany.

GUSTAV SCHROEDER *(to himself)*: What is going on? The Nazi government isn't usually so nice to Jews.

NARRATOR 1: Captain Schroeder calls a meeting of the ship's staff. He knows some Nazi party members are part of the crew, and he doesn't want them to make trouble. He makes them promise to treat the passengers with respect. Reluctantly, they agree. Finally, on May 13 passengers begin to board the ship. Among them are Dr. Fritz Spanier, his wife, Babette, and their seven-year-old twins, Inez and Renee. They walk up the gangplank in their most elegant clothes.

BABETTE SPANIER: At least we will leave Germany looking good!

FRITZ SPANIER: My brave Babette.

NARRATOR 1: At 8:00 P.M. the ship's horn blasts. Half an hour later, the captain receives a cable message from Claus-Gottfried Holthusen.

CLAUS-GOTTFRIED HOLTHUSEN: IMPERATIVE YOU MAKE ALL SPEED HAVANA . . . WHATEVER HAPPENS YOUR PASSENGERS WILL LAND. NO CAUSE FOR ALARM.

GUSTAV SCHROEDER: Something fishy is going on here. Why is Holthusen telling me to rush, but not to worry? Why did he wait until the ship left?

SCENE 2

NARRATOR 2: May 15. In Havana, Hamburg-America Line agent Luis Clasing meets with Manuel Benitez, Cuba's director of immigration.

LUIS CLASING: Here's five thousand dollars for you, Señor Benitez.

MANUEL BENITEZ: Are you trying to bribe me?

LUIS CLASING: Bribe you? Oh no, no, no, this is just a gift of appreciation.

MANUEL BENITEZ *(smiling)*: Of course! *(He slips the money into his pocket.)*

LUIS CLASING: But frankly, we do have a slight problem. Remember all those tourist visas you signed for the passengers on the *St. Louis*? And how they allow passengers to remain in Cuba while they look for some other country to take them? Well, I'm concerned about that new law, Decree 937, which President Bru signed. It forbids refugees to enter Cuba. Will he allow the *St. Louis* passengers to land?

MANUEL BENITEZ: Don't worry. It's just a piece of paper.

LUIS CLASING: I hope so. We don't want to return the passengers all the way back to Germany.

MANUEL BENITEZ: Calm down. I'll call President Bru right now.

NARRATOR 2: First, he meets with Cuba's secretary of state, Dr. Juan Remos.

MANUEL BENITEZ: You have to help me find a way around this Decree 937, Remos.

JUAN REMOS: I know all about your shady business. You've been using a loophole in Cuba's law to allow refugees in here.

MANUEL BENITEZ: Are you questioning my actions? I *am* the director of immigration!

JUAN REMOS: The visas you've been writing for the passengers are highly questionable.

MANUEL BENITEZ: What's wrong with them?

JUAN REMOS: You're admitting these passengers as tourists, and a person who can't go back to his own country is *not* a tourist. Besides, you're charging these poor people a fortune for these visas. Tell me, Benitez. How many of these have you written in the past few months?

MANUEL BENITEZ: Well, about four thousand.

JUAN REMOS: And how much do you charge for them?

MANUEL BENITEZ: Umm, well, one hundred fifty dollars each.

JUAN REMOS: And of course, the Hamburg-America Line is in on your little scheme, too. You sell them the visas, and they sell a package deal to desperate people: a visa for Cuba, and a cruise to get there. The whole thing is disgusting.

MANUEL BENITEZ: Why should those poor people escaping the Nazis suffer?

JUAN REMOS: Benitez, you're a real piece of work.

SCENE 3

NARRATOR 3: Tuesday, May 16 aboard the *St. Louis*. Evelyne and Renatta Aber roam the decks.

RENATTA ABER: I have a great idea! Let's rub soap on the doorknobs and see what happens!

EVELYNE ABER: Wouldn't that be naughty?

RENATTA ABER: Yes!

Read-Aloud Plays: World War II • Scholastic Teaching Resources

EVELYNE ABER: Then let's do it.

NARRATOR 3: After they play their prank, they hide and watch a steward stop at a cabin door, balancing a tray. He tries turning the handle, but his hand slips. The tray crashes down.

EVELYNE ABER: Ha ha!

RENATTA ABER: Ooh, look, string! Let's dangle it over the rail. And let it trail across and tickle the passengers dozing in chairs on the deck below.

EVELYNE ABER *(laughing)*: I like cruises! Lots of yummy food and lots of fun!

RENATTA ABER: Me too! I could stay here forever!

SCENE 4

NARRATOR 1: On May 23 Gustav Schroeder talks to his first officer.

GUSTAV SCHROEDER: Ostermeyer, listen to this cable I just got from Herr Holthusen. MAJORITY YOUR PASSENGERS IN CONTRAVENTION NEW CUBAN LAW 937 AND MAY NOT BE GIVEN PERMISSION DISEMBARK . . . What is this new law? As far as I know, our passengers' visas are all valid.

KLAUS OSTERMEYER: What will you do, Captain?

GUSTAV SCHROEDER: Let's form a passenger committee to deal with their worries.

NARRATOR 1: The committee of about five passengers meets later that day.

HERBERT MANASSE: Are we being sent back to Germany?

GUSTAV SCHROEDER: I promise I will do everything possible to avoid going back to Germany. I am only too well aware of what fate awaits you there.

SCENE 5

NARRATOR 2: Saturday, May 27. Over the past few days, the captain has sent two more cables to Holthusen, but has heard nothing. At 3:00 A.M. the ship reaches Cuba and drops anchors out in the harbor. In the morning, Clasing comes aboard.

GUSTAV SCHROEDER: What's going on?

LUIS CLASING: Relax. Everything will be fine.

GUSTAV SCHROEDER: Then why did you tell us to anchor out in the harbor?

LUIS CLASING: Captain, the ship has arrived. The passengers aren't your problem anymore.

GUSTAV SCHROEDER: These people are my responsibility until they are off this ship.

NARRATOR 2: Tuesday, May 30. The passengers have not been allowed to leave for two days. Now, the Nazi crewmembers have started harassing passengers. Some even become violent and beat people up. One passenger, Max Loewe, is so frightened he begins to go mad.

MAX LOEWE: I know there are Gestapo agents here, looking for me. They want to put me in a concentration camp!

ELISE LOEWE: Max, darling, please try to stay calm, for the children's sake.

NARRATOR 2: Frightened, Max Loewe sneaks off to hide. Later that afternoon, he slashes his wrists and throws himself into the harbor.

MAX LOEWE: They will never get me! Let me die!

OSKAR BLECHNER: Man overboard!

BRANDLA FLAMBERG: Someone, save him!

NARRATOR 2: A crewmember does and Loewe is taken to a Havana hospital. Newspapers write about Loewe's suicide attempt, saying that the *St. Louis* situation "shames the world." Demonstrations take place across the United States. In Germany, a Nazi paper says passengers should be sent to concentration camps.

SCENE 6

NARRATOR 3: Meanwhile, in Havana, President Frederico Bru meets with Remos.

JUAN REMOS: We already have about five thousand refugees. For our size, we have more refugees than almost any other country. Even though they aren't allowed to work, some get jobs—jobs they take from Cubans who need them.

FREDERICO BRU: Public opinion is swinging against the refugees, too.

JUAN REMOS: Nevertheless, there *is* a moral case for letting them in. And let's not forget America's opinion.

FREDERICO BRU: The United States doesn't want refugees either. I feel sorry for the refugees. However, sending the ship back to Germany is the lesser of two evils.

NARRATOR 3: Still, President Bru agrees to meet American lawyer Lawrence Berenson on June 1. Berenson has been sent to Cuba by the American Jewish Joint Distribution Committee in New York.

LAWRENCE BERENSON: Isn't there any way we can persuade you to let the refugees stay? For example, could the passengers stay on the Isle of Pines, off the coast of Cuba?

FREDERICO BRU: I won't negotiate until the *St. Louis* has left Cuban waters.

LAWRENCE BERENSON (*to himself*)**:** He might . . . if we offer him enough money.

NARRATOR 3: Over the next few days, through discussions with government officials, Berenson learns that the Cuban government might let refugees in––for five hundred dollars per refugee. He talks to Joseph Hyman, executive director of the American Jewish Joint Distribution Committee.

LAWRENCE BERENSON: I think I can work out a deal with him to let them back in.

JOSEPH HYMAN: What sort of deal?

LAWRENCE BERENSON: Maybe if we pay him enough money, Bru will change his mind.

SCENE 7

NARRATOR 1: Meanwhile, Captain Schroeder gets orders to leave Havana. On June 2 the *St. Louis* is forced to leave Havana at 11:02 A.M. The next day, the passenger committee sends cables begging the United States to admit them. However, the United States decides against it. The country is recovering from ten years of the Depression and thirty million people are unemployed. Though most Americans dislike the Nazis, they do not want Europe's refugees. The ship's purser, Ferdinand Mueller, meets with Captain Schroeder.

FERDINAND MUELLER: Sir, I'm worried. We will run out of food and water in about twelve days. We have to land passengers soon.

GUSTAV SCHROEDER: You're right. If we don't, they might stage a revolt.

SCENE 8

NARRATOR 2: Berenson meets with Bru again.

FREDERICO BRU: Can you meet our demands?

LAWRENCE BERENSON: I hope so, sir. We're doing our best to raise the money.

FREDERICO BRU: By the way, I don't just want five hundred dollars per passenger. I want an extra one hundred fifty thousand–dollar bond to make sure that they don't cost the government anything while they live on the Isle of Pines. Furthermore, my demands must be met in full within forty-eight hours.

NARRATOR 2: Later, Berenson talks to Joseph Hyman.

LAWRENCE BERENSON: Bru is demanding more than six hundred thousand dollars. How can we raise that much money?

JOSEPH HYMAN: I will send as much cash to Cuba as I can, but try to negotiate, okay? Any money you save can be spent on helping other refugees.

LAWRENCE BERENSON: Of course. Have you tried seeing if any other countries will take them?

JOSEPH HYMAN: So far, Venezuela, Ecuador, Chile, Colombia, Paraguay, and Argentina have all said no. So has Canada, and I hold out no hope for the United States. Cuba's our best shot.

NARRATOR 2: Berenson returns to his hotel.

LAWRENCE BERENSON (*to himself*)**:** They can't be serious about their price. I'll offer them four hundred forty-three thousand dollars. Surely that will be enough. If not, Bru can ask for more.

NARRATOR 2: But the next day, Berenson gets a message: The Cuban government has rejected his offer. Berenson calls Joseph Hyman.

LAWRENCE BERENSON: I hoped to negotiate, but Bru wasn't interested.

JOSEPH HYMAN: We'll get the money somehow. Tell Bru we'll give him the full amount. We must save those people.

NARRATOR 2: But the Cuban government says it is too late.

SCENE 9

NARRATOR 3: That evening, the Captain gets orders to return to Hamburg immediately. After turning the ship toward Europe, he calls for a meeting of all passengers.

GUSTAV SCHROEDER: We are returning to Europe. I have waited as long as possible, hoping the situation would change. But we're short of food. We're short of fuel. We could only hold out for about a week before we'd be forced into port anyway. We'll have to keep hoping for a solution.

AARON POZNER: We must not go to Germany! They'll stick us all in concentration camps.

FRITZ SPANIER: What is truly maddening is how this plays right into the Nazis' hand. How can the world criticize Germany for its treatment of Jews when other countries reject them?

HERBERT MANASSE: Silence! Ladies and gentlemen, the news *is* bad. But Europe is still many days away. That gives all our friends time to make new moves to help us. Let's get busy sending cables to European governments. Surely, someone will help us.

GUSTAV SCHROEDER: I now believe you should pin your hopes on Great Britain.

SCENE 10

NARRATOR 1: One afternoon, steward Leo Jockl talks to Aaron Pozner.

LEO JOCKL: May I ask what is it like being a Jew in Germany these days?

AARON POZNER: It's not easy. I was in a concentration camp for a year. I was beaten. I saw people killed. I had to flee my home, leaving my family behind.

Read-Aloud Plays: World War II • Scholastic Teaching Resources

LEO JOCKL: But have you never lost your faith?

AARON POZNER: No, I have not lost my faith, but only a Jew would understand why.

NARRATOR 1: As Pozner leaves, he feels guilty for having said that to Jockl.

AARON POZNER (*meeting Jockl later*)**:** I'm sorry I was rude to you before. Can I ask you a question? Are *you* Jewish?

LEO JOCKL: Um, excuse me, I must leave.

NARRATOR 2: In fact, Aaron Pozner was on to something. Leo Jockl also faced his own threat.

GUSTAV SCHROEDER: The Nazis cabled me. They want to know if you're Jewish.

LEO JOCKL: Sir, you and I both know I am half-Jewish. Will you tell them my secret?

GUSTAV SCHROEDER: Of course not. God help us both if they discover the truth.

NARRATOR 2: On Friday, June 9, Leo Jockl goes to visit Aaron Pozner, but finds his cabin empty. Crushed cigarettes cover the floor. He goes to the captain.

LEO JOCKL: I'm worried. It looks as if there's been some kind of meeting. Aaron warned that he might try to take over the ship.

GUSTAV SCHROEDER: Find him, Jockl, before he does anything foolish.

NARRATOR 3: At 4:30 P.M. Pozner and other passengers take over the ship's bridge.

GUSTAV SCHROEDER: Why are you doing this?

AARON POZNER: We're keeping this ship away from Germany!

GUSTAV SCHROEDER: Stop this immediately, or you'll be charged with piracy.

AARON POZNER: Then we'll hold you hostage.

GUSTAV SCHROEDER: Pozner, you are behaving like a criminal. However, I will overlook that if you leave this bridge in one minute.

NARRATOR 3: He turns his back on them.

AARON POZNER: Captain, please. We can't return to Germany.

GUSTAV SCHROEDER: I will do everything possible to land the passengers in England.

AARON POZNER: If you promise.

GUSTAV SCHROEDER (*later, to himself*)**:** If worse comes to worse, I'll run the *St. Louis* close to England, set the ship on fire, and evacuate the passengers ashore. We can't go to Germany!

SCENE 11

NARRATOR 1: But finally, when all hope seems lost, the passengers get a break. All the cables, the news stories, and international efforts pay off. The head of the Jewish refugee committee in Paris, France, makes certain phone calls. On Saturday, June 10, Belgium offers to take two hundred passengers. On June 13, three more countries—France, Holland, and Great Britain—agree to take all of the remaining passengers. On June 13, the captain calls a meeting.

GUSTAV SCHROEDER: Well, ladies and gentlemen, good news. Here's a cable from the European director of the Jewish Joint Distribution Committee in Paris: FINAL ARRANGEMENTS FOR DISEMBARKATION ALL PASSENGERS COMPLETE. GOVERNMENTS OF BELGIUM, HOLLAND, FRANCE, AND ENGLAND COOPERATED MAGNIFICENTLY.

BABETTE SPANIER: We're saved! We're saved!

OSKAR BLECHNER: But where will each of us be going?

BRANDLA FLAMBERG: That's a good question! Can you tell us, Mr. Joseph?

JOSEF JOSEPH: Let's see . . . . According to this list, I believe you will be going to England, Mr. Blechner. Mrs. Flamberg, you and your daughter, Fella, will stop in Belgium. And Mrs. Spanier, your family's destination is Holland.

GUSTAV SCHROEDER: We can sort all this out later. In the meantime, let's celebrate!

JOSEF JOSEPH: Captain, our gratitude is as immense as the ocean on which we have been traveling since May 13.

EPILOGUE

NARRATOR 1: The passengers all got new homes. But by the next year, the Nazis had swept through France, Holland, and Belgium. Most of the *St. Louis* passengers were forced into concentration camps. By the end of the war, fewer than a third of the men, women, and children who sailed on the *St. Louis* had survived.

Background on the Jewish Refugee Flight

A Worsening Climate: After the Nazis took power in the early 1930s, life for Jews in Germany deteriorated. In February 1935, the Nazi government said that Jews were no longer considered German citizens. Over the next five years, Jews were expelled from schools, government jobs, and often their homes. They were publicly humiliated and forced to wear yellow stars. In November 1938, the Nazis led a two-night campaign of terror called *Kristallnacht*, smashing windows of Jewish homes and businesses, looting, and destroying synagogues. They attacked and beat Jews, killing more than 91. More than 26,000 people, including Aaron Pozner, were arrested and thrown into concentration camps. After this attack, many Jews were desperate to leave Germany. Before the war, though Hitler was publicly toying with the idea of letting Jews leave Europe for resettlement elsewhere, it was difficult to do so. Later, he instituted his "Final Solution"—trying to rid the world of Jewish people through institutionalized mass murder. Millions of Jews—and others—were killed in this horrifying era.

The Passengers' Fate: According to one estimate, of the 907 *St. Louis* passengers who returned to Europe, only 240 were alive at the end of the war. Here's what happened to some of them:

• Josef Joseph and his family lived in England and later moved to New York.

• The Spanier family spent five years in Westerbork Concentration Camp in the Netherlands, where Fritz Spanier was forced to work as a camp doctor.

• Max Loewe died in 1942 from heart disease. His family survived.

• Herbert Manasse was killed fleeing the Nazis.

• Aaron Pozner was killed in a concentration camp at Auschwitz.

Life wasn't easy for the crew of the *St. Louis*, either. Leo Jockl was killed on November 17, 1944, while being used as a human minesweeper by the Nazis. He was strafed by Allied bullets fired from a plane. Both Purser Mueller and First Officer Ostermeyer lived through the war, but were captured by the Russians. For many years they lived in Communist East Germany. After returning the *St. Louis* to Germany, Captain Schroeder stopped being a captain. He worked at a desk job. When the war ended, he had a hard time making a living. Some of the passengers helped him by sending him money, food, and clothes. The West German government gave him a medal in 1959 to honor him for trying to save the passengers.

CRITICAL THINKING

★ Helpless

Many of the passengers on the *St. Louis* reported feeling helpless and trapped as they drifted around in the Atlantic. Ask students: *Have you ever had situations in which you felt helpless and trapped? How did you cope with those feelings? How would you advise someone else who feels helpless to deal with his or her emotions?*

★ Prejudice

Some Germans were prejudiced against the Jews. Others, like Captain Schroeder, were not. Ask: *What factors might have influenced their attitudes to their fellow citizens? Why are some people prejudiced and some not? Upbringing? Circumstance? Can people be manipulated into feeling prejudice and hatred for people they otherwise would not? If so, then why do some people resist feeling hatred while others give in to it?*

★ Leaving Home

Before the war, most German Jews considered themselves full German citizens. Many served as soldiers in World War I and their families lived and worked there for generations. Ask: *How would you feel if you had to leave your home and move to another country? What would you miss? What would you look forward to? How would you adjust? What would be the hardest part of leaving your homeland? Who in your family would have the easiest or hardest time? Why? What might you learn from making such a change? Would it be a positive or negative experience?*

ACTIVITIES

★ Remember Human Rights

Like the passengers on the *St. Louis*, the rights of Jews and many other people were violated during World War II. Violations of human rights still take place around the world today. Encourage students to find out more about current human rights issues by contacting Amnesty International. Through this group, your class can also write to government officials on behalf of people around the world who are held as political prisoners. To learn about Amnesty International, you can visit them on the Internet at www.amnestyusa.org, write to them at Amnesty International USA, 322 8th Avenue, New York, NY 10001, or call (212) 807-8400.

★ Welcome to America?

Each year, millions of people want to come to the United States. Some are desperate refugees. Others want to come for the better opportunities that can be found in our wealthy nation. What would the United States be like if it admitted every refugee who wanted to enter? Divide the class into two halves. Stage a debate between one team who favors admitting the *St. Louis* passengers, and the other who opposes allowing them into the United States. A few questions to consider: *Is it fair for the United States to admit every person who wants to come? What effect might admitting large numbers of immigrants have on the job market? What is the fairest way to decide who can come to this country? Should it be based on need or urgency, or on who can contribute skills or money?*

★ *St. Louis* Calendar

Help students organize their understanding of what happened on the *St. Louis* by arranging the events in chronological order. Take two pieces of paper. Make up calendar grids (five rows of seven boxes across) for the months of May and June 1939. (Note: May 1, 1939, started on a Monday, while June 1 started on a Thursday.) Then make enough photocopies for the class. Have students examine the play and write down on their calendars what happened on which day. Once students have filled in their calendar grids, they can use the information and dates to write their own diary from the point of view of a child on the *St. Louis*. Ask them to write how they feel about leaving their lives in Germany, about what life is like aboard ship, and how their emotions shift over the course of the journey.

★ Persuasive Writing

The passengers on the *St. Louis* cabled influential leaders, newspaper editors, and famous people to try to get their help in finding a new home for the ship's passengers. Have students write their own cables to ask leaders to allow them to land in Cuba. Remind them to try to use persuasive language and compelling arguments to make their case.

Note: This play was created with the help of books, newspaper and magazine articles, and Web sites. The following resources were particularly helpful:
Voyage of the Damned by Gordon Thomas and
     Max Morgan Witts (Stein and Day, 1974)
U.S. Holocaust Memorial Museum
     Voyage of the St. Louis
     **http://www.ushmm.org/
     outreach/louis.htm**
American-Israeli Cooperative Enterprise
     **http:// www.us-israel.org/jsource/
     Holocaust/stlouis.html**

In the Blitz

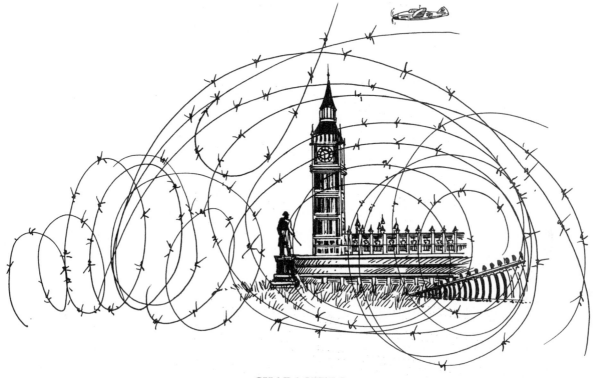

CHARACTERS

*TOM PARSONS, *age 11*

*MR. MICHAEL PARSONS

*MRS. URSULA PARSONS

*JOE PARSONS, *age 10*

*MAGGIE PARSONS, *age 14*

*MRS. HILARY HEATH, *evacuation organizer*

*MISS CLAIRE EAMES, *Essex County resident*

*MRS. EVELYN CALDWELL, *the Parsonses' neighbor*

*MR. NIGEL CALDWELL, *the Parsonses' neighbor*

WINSTON CHURCHILL, *Britain's Prime Minister*

*VICKY CALDWELL, *age 18*

*ACCORDION PLAYER

NARRATORS 1–3

*denotes fictional characters

SCENE 1

NARRATOR 1: It is September 3, 1939. The Parsons family gathers around the radio in their suburban London home. Great Britain's Prime Minister has just declared war against Germany after Hitler invaded Poland.

TOM PARSONS: What does this mean, Dad?

MICHAEL PARSONS: The Germans may try to attack us, just as they attacked Poland, so we have to prepare for war.

URSULA PARSONS: At least the government's given every citizen a gas mask.

MICHAEL PARSONS: Let's just hope that we're so well prepared that "Jerry" won't even bother trying to use gas on us.

SCENE 2

NARRATOR 2: A few weeks later, a truck drops off a load of corrugated steel at the Parsonses' house. The family gathers in the backyard to look at it.

JOE PARSONS: What's this for?

MICHAEL PARSONS: We're going to build an Anderson shelter in our backyard.

URSULA PARSONS: You aren't going to dig up my roses for that nasty thing, are you?

MICHAEL PARSONS: I just do what the government tells me to. Which reminds me, I've volunteered to be a warden. I want to set an example.

JOE PARSONS: A warden? What's that?

MICHAEL PARSONS: I'll patrol two or three blocks, enforce the blackouts and things like that. If there's bomb damage, it will be my job to report it.

TOM PARSONS: Can I help build the shelter, Dad?

MICHAEL PARSONS: Of course.

NARRATOR 2: They dig a hole, fill it with corrugated metal, and put up another wall. Then they cover the top with dirt and large tree branches.

MAGGIE PARSONS: Doesn't it need a proper door? You just make a doorway with a piece of cloth and some sandbags?

MICHAEL PARSONS: Bombs might make a regular door splinter. That could really hurt us.

MAGGIE PARSONS (*imagining the explosion*)**:** How awful!

TOM PARSONS: Oh, Mum, it's lovely. It's just like a playhouse.

MICHAEL PARSONS: I'll put bunks along the sides, and we can camp out here if we have to. Pull more of those sandbags out of here, would you, Tom?

Read-Aloud Plays: World War II • Scholastic Teaching Resources

MAGGIE PARSONS: I still think it needs a proper door.

NARRATOR 2: A few weeks later at the Parsonses' home.

URSULA PARSONS: I just heard that the children are to be evacuated to the country in the next month or so. I suppose it is too dangerous for them to stay here. Besides, fresh air will do them good.

MAGGIE PARSONS: But what about you and Dad?

URSULA PARSONS: There isn't room for everyone in the countryside. Now, Maggie, mind you, watch the boys.

MAGGIE PARSONS: I will, Mum.

SCENE 3

NARRATOR 3: A few days later, the children get their orders to evacuate. The family gathers at the train station before the children leave.

URSULA PARSONS: I expect you to write all the time, d'you hear? I'm still your mother!

TOM PARSONS: Oh, Mum! Don't get all soppy on us.

MICHAEL PARSONS: They're right, Ursula. They'll settle down in no time, you'll see.

URSULA PARSONS: Right you are, darling. Chin up. We must be brave. Let's see, you've got everything . . . suitcase, identity card, gas mask. . . . Let me kiss you all then.

JOE PARSONS: Oh, all right. That's enough, Mum! People are looking.

NARRATOR 3: They get on the train and look out the window. As the train pulls out of the station, there are tears welling up in the Parsons children's eyes. After a few hours, they get to a small town in the county of Essex.

JOE PARSONS: Look, the Cub Scouts are handing out tea and Marmite sandwiches. It can't be so bad.

HILARY HEATH: Now line up, children.

NARRATOR 3: People from town choose the children they want to keep with them. Finally, only the Parsons children are left.

HILARY HEATH: Will no one take these three children?

CLAIRE EAMES: Three! That's a lot of children. Oh, all right then. I will, if I must.

HILARY HEATH: Thank you, Miss Eames.

CLAIRE EAMES (to the children)**:** If you're going to stay at my house, you'd better be neat. You know how to wipe your feet before you come in, don't you?

TOM, JOE, AND MAGGIE PARSONS: Yes, Miss.

CLAIRE EAMES: I don't like dirty habits.

NARRATOR 3: They settle into their routine at Miss Eameses' house for the next few weeks. One afternoon Tom and Joe are in the kitchen.

TOM PARSONS: Look, jam tarts!

CLAIRE EAMES (coming into the room)**:** Those aren't for you, boys. The vicar's coming for tea. Now go wash up.

NARRATOR 3: A little later, they sneak into the kitchen again.

JOE PARSONS: They look so good.

TOM PARSONS: You don't suppose she'd miss just one, do you? We could share one. Surely the vicar can't eat all twelve.

NARRATOR 3: As Tom reaches for a tart, he accidentally knocks over the tray.

CLAIRE EAMES (coming into the room)**:** Boys! How could you do such a thing when there's a shortage of sugar and butter! Go up to your room, and don't expect any supper!

MAGGIE PARSONS (following her into the kitchen)**:** Oh, Miss Eames, please don't be so hard on my brothers.

CLAIRE EAMES: If someone doesn't punish them, how will they learn?

NARRATOR 3: Tom writes a letter home.

TOM PARSONS: "Dear Mum, Please save us. Miss Eames is quite mean. Love, Tom."

NARRATOR 3: A few days later, Mrs. Parsons appears at the home of Miss Eames.

URSULA PARSONS: I'm taking them home.

CLAIRE EAMES: If you think that's best.

PARSONS CHILDREN (on the train back to London)**:** Thank you, Mum.

URSULA PARSONS: You *were* very naughty, children. I'm sure Miss Eames tried, but perhaps she isn't used to children. Still, I would have come in any case. I saw the posters everywhere: "Don't do it, Mother—Leave the children where they are." But I can't help it. I want you with me. Families belong together. Whatever we face, we'll do it together.

SCENE 4

NARRATOR 1: On January 28, 1940, rationing begins in Britain.

EVELYN CALDWELL: Look, coupon books. We'll have to use these when we buy everything: clothes, sugar, meat . . .

Read-Aloud Plays: World War II • Scholastic Teaching Resources

NIGEL CALDWELL: At least the rich won't have everything while the rest of us starve.

MICHAEL PARSONS: We must all do our share in wartime.

NARRATOR 1: They watch as the war intensifies across Europe. Having captured Finland and Poland, the Nazis invade Denmark and Norway on April 9.

EVELYN CALDWELL: Hitler is a madman! What will he do next?

MICHAEL PARSONS: You'd be amazed at how many people think it won't happen here.

MAGGIE PARSONS: But we already get air attacks. I saw a dogfight just last Tuesday.

MICHAEL PARSONS: When I go out on my rounds, reminding people to keep their black-out curtains from letting any light out, some people tell me I'm a busybody!

NARRATOR 1: In May, Germany attacks Belgium and the Netherlands.

MICHAEL PARSONS: Look, kids, I've got the map from the *Daily Express* on the wall. We can put these little flag pins to keep track of the war. So far, we aren't doing well.

JOE PARSONS: Father, listen to the wireless!

URSULA PARSONS (*from the kitchen*)**:** What does it say?

MICHAEL PARSONS: Rotterdam, Holland, has fallen into Nazi hands.

MAGGIE PARSONS: Why doesn't America help? Don't they realize that sooner or later, the Axis powers are going to attack them too?

MICHAEL PARSONS: They're doing something at least, sending supplies and weapons across the Atlantic with their merchant marines.

URSULA PARSONS: We can't win this war alone. All of Europe is falling to Hitler.

MAGGIE PARSONS: And what will happen to our troops there if France falls?

NARRATOR 1: Soon, Hitler attacks France. Within days, France is forced to surrender. On June 2, more than three hundred and thirty-five thousand Allied forces withdraw from the beaches of Dunkirk, France, back to England. Winston Churchill, Britain's new Prime Minister, gives a speech and the entire nation listens.

WINSTON CHURCHILL: Let us therefore brace ourselves to our duty and so bear ourselves that if the British Empire and its Commonwealth lasts for a thousand years men will still say, "This was their finest hour."

EVELYN CALDWELL: Well, we're all alone now.

TOM PARSONS: You know what Winston Churchill says. If they attack, you fight back. Maybe they'll kill you, but you can always take one with you.

JOE PARSONS: Good old Winnie!

SCENE 5

NARRATOR 2: Late August. Air battles between the British Royal Air Force (RAF) and German fighters have become more intense and frequent in recent months. Though they are vastly outnumbered, the British are helped by a new invention called radar, which helps them detect incoming German planes. In the Parsonses' neighborhood, people stand outside watching one plane chasing another.

URSULA PARSONS: What kind of plane is that?

MAGGIE PARSONS: It's a German one—a Dornier, I think. With one of our Spitfires behind it.

NIGEL CALDWELL: Come on, lad! Get him! Get him!

JOE PARSONS: Come on, you can do it!

TOM PARSONS: Hey, you pilot! Get the Nazi! Get him!

MAGGIE PARSONS: He's gaining on him!

NARRATOR 2: Suddenly, the German plane bursts into flames and falls toward a nearby field.

JOE AND TOM PARSONS: He did it! He did it!

URSULA PARSONS: That's one less Nazi to worry about.

NARRATOR 2: The air war intensifies by late August.

JOE PARSONS: Mum, why do you look so worried?

URSULA PARSONS: The Nazis knocked out our most important airfield. If they knock out all of our major RAF airfields, Britain will be defenseless. Then the Nazis could invade.

MICHAEL PARSONS: They've got more planes than we have, but they haven't got our spirit.

URSULA PARSONS: We'll never live under Hitler! Never!

NARRATOR 2: One evening, Vicky Caldwell comes outside and joins the Parsons on the street.

URSULA PARSONS: Why Vicky, don't you look smart in that uniform!

VICKY CALDWELL: I'm training to be an ambulance driver.

MICHAEL PARSONS: Aren't you brave!

VICKY CALDWELL: A lot of brave boys are risking their lives. I want to help too.

URSULA PARSONS: You're a modern woman, Vicky. I like that.

MAGGIE PARSONS: I can't wait till I'm an ambulance driver too.

Read-Aloud Plays: World War II • Scholastic Teaching Resources

URSULA PARSONS: We'll see, dear. Let's hope we've knocked out Hitler before that.

SCENE 6

NARRATOR 3: On September 7, Hitler sends far more planes than ever before. This time, the Nazis don't aim for military targets. They try to attack civilians. The Germans call this *Blitzkrieg*—"lightning war." They start with an attack on East London. When it's over, neighbors come over to talk with the Parsons.

URSULA PARSONS: Look at the orange sky over to the east. It's so beautiful, and so terrible.

NIGEL CALDWELL: They say that huge warehouse fires broke out in the East End.

URSULA PARSONS: How dreadful!

MICHAEL PARSONS: I heard on the wireless that hundreds were injured, and they were sent to a school. While they were there, the school was bombed. Hundreds more got killed.

EVELYN CALDWELL: Oh dear, poor East Enders. Now the war seems so real!

NIGEL CALDWELL: I know the London docks are full of factories and warehouses that the Germans would want to bomb. But why hit poor people's houses?

NARRATOR 3: The bombing continues night after night. Later that month . . .

EVELYN CALDWELL: Did you hear the news? The Germans bombed Buckingham Palace!

TOM PARSONS: Oh, no! How are the king and queen?

URSULA PARSONS: Tom, are you eavesdropping again?

EVELYN CALDWELL: Oh, it's quite all right. They're fine. But it was a close one. They were only 80 yards away. Luckily, their window was already open, or they probably would have been killed by flying glass.

NIGEL CALDWELL: I hear that they're going around the East End with the Princesses Elizabeth and Margaret Rose. You know what the queen said? She said she felt almost glad she was bombed, because now she could finally look East London in the face.

EVELYN CALDWELL: Good for her! She could have taken herself and the princesses to Canada for safety, but they're going to stick it out here, I read.

MAGGIE PARSONS: Then God save the king and queen, and the princesses, too.

NARRATOR 3: Night after night, the Blitz continues over London. During the month of October, attacks are at their heaviest. All over London friends and neighbors gather together to talk.

EVELYN CALDWELL: Yawning again, I see, Ursula.

URSULA PARSONS: I can't help it. It's impossible to sleep in the Anderson shelter every night, with those bombs going off, the sirens, and the worry. It's been every night for a month!

EVELYN CALDWELL: How can the blackouts do any good? It's dreadful. The incendiary bombs start fires, and then the Germans just look for the fires and try to do more damage.

MICHAEL PARSONS: That's why the firefighters are our best line of defense.

EVELYN CALDWELL: And even if a bomb is a few blocks away, you don't know if it's going to knock out the electricity or the water.

URSULA PARSONS: Half the time, school is cancelled, so the children are underfoot. Even if they do go, I can't help but worry about them.

EVELYN CALDWELL: Cooking is so difficult when we can't get basic ingredients. One day, I waited for four hours on line to get a few bananas.

URSULA PARSONS: Speaking of shopping, I'm going into the city to shop now. There's hardly a thing to eat in the house. Want to come along?

EVELYN CALDWELL: Not today, thanks.

URSULA PARSONS: Perhaps we can get some sausages or some whale meat.

JOE PARSONS: I don't like the whale, Mummy! It tastes all fishy.

URSULA PARSONS: Oh, it's not so bad if I soak it in vinegar overnight, is it?

JOE PARSONS: Then it's all vinegary.

URSULA PARSONS: Well, I can get nice big cuts of it for cheap, and I must feed you children something.

SCENE 7

NARRATOR 1: Joe and his mother ride into the city and wait in a long line at a fish store.

JOE PARSONS: Remember what the poster says, Mummy. "Don't take the Squander Bug when you go shopping."

URSULA PARSONS: I can hardly squander anything when there's almost nothing to buy, Joe.

JOE PARSONS (listening)**:** Oh no! The sirens are wailing again. It's another air raid!

URSULA PARSONS: We haven't time to get home. We'd better find a shelter.

JOE PARSONS: There's a tube station right over there, Mum.

URSULA PARSONS: Let's run for it.

NARRATOR 1: They hurry to the nearest station of the London Underground.

JOE PARSONS *(entering the station)***:** It's so crowded.

URSULA PARSONS: Let's see if we can find a little room for ourselves.

JOE PARSONS: Oooh, Mummy, may I please, please, please, have money to buy sweets from the confectionery machine?

URSULA PARSONS: I'm sorry, Joe. I haven't much extra money with me.

ACCORDION PLAYER: Here are some pence for the boy. Let him have a little treat.

JOE PARSONS: Thank you, sir.

URSULA PARSONS: We can't take that, sir.

ACCORDION PLAYER: Please let me give it to him, Ma'am. We all have to help each other now.

URSULA PARSONS: Well, then, thank you, sir. It's a pity it took a war to bring us together and give us that Blitz Spirit, but at least we are together now.

NARRATOR 1: The old man starts playing his accordion. Soon, everyone is singing popular songs. They end with a patriotic tune.

ACCORDION PLAYER *(singing)***:** "Rule Britannia/Britannia rule the Waves,/Britons never, never, never/Shall be slaves."

NARRATOR 1: Afterward, everyone lies down on the concrete floor. People spread their coats on top of themselves.

URSULA PARSONS: Your father will worry. But we're safe for now.

JOE PARSONS: Mum, I'm scared.

NARRATOR 1: She hugs him tight as another bomb falls close by, shaking dust down from the ceiling. The bombing keeps up through the night. They don't return home until the next day. Their worried family greets them with relief.

SCENE 8

NARRATOR 2: Over the next few months, the Germans concentrate on attacking other cities in Britain. But danger still remains in London. One day, Maggie is walking home from school with Tom and Joe.

TOM PARSONS *(covering his ears)***:** Oh no, air sirens! Not again!

MAGGIE PARSONS: We've got to get home. Run!

NARRATOR 2: Bombs are exploding, and they hear the whine of aircraft coming toward them. They flatten themselves against a wall as bullets ping down the street close by. Then they huddle behind a small shed nearby until the "All Clear" siren is sounded. After they reemerge, they see flattened silvery bullets all down the road. They start picking them up and putting them in their pockets.

TOM PARSONS: Are you all right then, Joe? You look a bit shaky.

JOE PARSONS: I'm *fine*. And look—shrapnel!

TOM PARSONS: Brilliant! Now we'll get pockets full of shrapnel to add to our collection!

SCENE 9

NARRATOR 3: That night, the air raid sirens wail again. The Parsons grab their blankets and head for their Anderson shelter.

URSULA PARSONS: Surely they can't keep this up for long.

MICHAEL PARSONS: Look what happened to Rotterdam.

URSULA PARSONS: Well, we are not going to submit! We just aren't!

MICHAEL PARSONS: I like your fighting spirit, dear!

MAGGIE PARSONS: Listen to that bomber. It sounds as if it's going to pass over us again . . . one, two, three. Oh no, it's . . .

NARRATOR 3: *Blammm!* They hear a huge blast.

MICHAEL PARSONS: Are you all okay?

URSULA PARSONS: Yes, but I'm not sure about the house.

NARRATOR 3: Through the shelter's curtains, they see the windows smashed in Tom and Joe's room. When the "All Clear" sounds, they go upstairs and see dust and glass everywhere.

URSULA PARSONS: What a mess. But you were right, Michael, about building that Anderson shelter.

TOM PARSONS: Oh, no!

MICHAEL PARSONS: What's wrong?

TOM PARSONS: The Nazis wrecked my collection of Aircraft of the RAF trading cards.

JOE PARSONS: And they got my shrapnel collection.

MICHAEL PARSONS: Somehow I don't think you'll have trouble starting a new one. Well, I suppose we'd best clean up this mess as much as we can. Don't cut yourselves on the glass.

Read-Aloud Plays: World War II • Scholastic Teaching Resources

NARRATOR 3: That night, the whole family tries to go to sleep in the living room.

TOM PARSONS: Joe, are you awake?

JOE PARSONS: Yes.

TOM PARSONS: What are you thinking about?

JOE PARSONS: I was just thinking, if a bomber comes and strafes us with machine gun fire, is it better to run or to play dead?

TOM PARSONS: Play dead, definitely.

JOE PARSONS: Oh, don't be daft. Running is definitely better.

MICHAEL PARSONS: Children, go to sleep.

TOM PARSONS: Mum?

URSULA PARSONS: Yes, Tom?

TOM PARSONS: Do you think we'll win the war? I mean, really?

URSULA PARSONS: I think so, Tom. If we all try to stay tremendously brave and strong, and stick together, then I hope so. I think so.

JOE PARSONS: Good-night then, Mum.

URSULA PARSONS: Good-night, children.

EPILOGUE

NARRATOR 1: The Blitz continued until late into the spring of 1941. The Nazis believed that the British would be so terrified by the bombings that they would surrender to Nazi control. But the British refused to give in, and finally, Hitler sent the bulk of his air forces to Eastern Europe, in the fight for control of Russia. Britain would be bombed again— and families like the Parsons faced years of hardships during the war—but the attacks would never be as intense as they were during the Blitz.

Background on the War in England

Blitzkrieg: The word means "lightning war." The Germans meant for their lightning-like attacks on their foes to be swift, devastating, and overwhelming. They hoped to fill the people of Britain with such fear and despair that they would surrender. After all, the Netherlands fell to German control after the city of Rotterdam was pummeled by an intense bombing campaign. The strategy, however, did not work in Britain. For one thing, Britain was an island, and its physical separation from Europe's mainland made it more difficult to invade. Another factor was the fierce will of the British people. Because Britain had not been invaded for nearly a thousand years, the resolve of its people to resist surrender was only strengthened by the attacks.

Pulling Together: One factor that helped breed unity among the British was the sense of shared sacrifice. Though inequities remained, Britain's people cooperated with each other to a remarkable degree. They volunteered as wardens, ambulance drivers, farm workers, and soldiers. They shared their homes with bombed-out neighbors, city children, and others in need. They willingly accepted rationing limits with little complaint. Their practical, plucky attitude won the admiration of the world.

For the Sake of the Children: The Blitz changed the lives of children. More than a million and a half children left Britain's cities in advance of the invasion. Some went to Canada, Australia, and other countries. Most went to the countryside. But though the intention behind the plan to send children away was a humane one —to save children's lives—it had other negative effects, such as separating families.

A High Cost: From September 1939, when it started, until May 1940, when it ended, the Blitz was devastating to London and other British cities. In some parts of London, as many as 80 percent of the homes were damaged or destroyed. Precious landmarks like the House of Commons and Coventry Cathedral were damaged. The human cost was very high as well. German attacks during the Blitz caused more than 90,000 casualties, including between 15,000 and 50,000 deaths.

CRITICAL THINKING

★ Blitz Spirit

During the Blitz, many people in Britain noted that there was a very special "Blitz Spirit." People helped each other as never before. Ask students: *How do you think people treated each other after the war ended? Do you think it is likely that a spirit of national unity and a willingness to look out for one's neighbor would have lasted in peacetime? Why or why not?*

★ Evacuations

Thousands of children, like the Parsons children in this play, were separated from their families at some point during the Blitz. Ask students: *How would you feel if you were in this situation? Which would be a better choice for you in a time of serious danger— going to a safe place without your family, or staying with your family no matter how dangerous it was? What would be the advantages and disadvantages of each alternative?*

★ Resilience

During the war, children found themselves in a variety of horrible situations. Ask students: *How did children learn to cope? In this play, did the war seem worse for the grown-ups or for the children? Explain your answer.*

ACTIVITIES

★ Loose Lips Sink Ships

In the play, characters discuss various posters they see around them. For example, Joe remarks on a poster about the "Squander Bug." Throughout the war, posters in train stations, bus kiosks, and other places urged Britons (and in the United States, Americans) to cooperate with the war effort in various ways, from keeping secrets to avoiding waste to drinking lots of milk and observing curfews. After reading this play, have the class do library research to learn more about the Blitz. Have students make their own posters to support the war effort, using some of these themes and others that seem appropriate. Then display them around the classroom.

★ Making Do

During the Blitz, money and other resources were tight. Children had to make their own fun—and often, their own toys. They would fashion tops out of lemonade bottle caps and toy cars from old cans. Bring in some simple, recyclable materials, such as cereal boxes, plastic bottles, bottle caps, and string, as well as tape, glue, scissors, and so on. Have students try making their own toys, such as cars, planes, dolls, packs of playing cards, and whatever else they can think of.

★ Music

During the height of the Blitz, people would cheer themselves up by singing popular or patriotic songs, such as "The White Cliffs of Dover" and "Rule Britannia." Discuss how music can bring people together in a scary time. Ask students if there are songs that are significant to the era they live in. Have students pretend they are living during the Blitz. Have them gather in groups to make up their own songs to boost wartime spirit.

They can use the tunes of traditional songs and make up their own lyrics. Or, if they want, they can create a rap instead. Then they can present their songs to the class.

★ Dear Cousin

Have students pretend they are British children writing letters to a cousin who now lives in the United States. Have them talk about their daily lives. How has life changed since the war started? What do they do for fun? How do they feel when bombs are overhead? What comforts did they have? What kinds of things are hardest to bear? Give them extra points for using vivid detail.

★ Good Old Winnie

British Prime Minister Winston Churchill was one of history's greatest wartime leaders. His stirring speeches and his resolute manner helped the British cope with hard times during the war. Have students learn more about Winston Churchill. They can create their own plays or biographies about this important man and share them with the class.

Pearl Harbor

CHARACTERS

CORDELL HULL, *U.S. secretary of state* • KICHISABURO NOMURA, *Japanese ambassador*

GENERAL HIDEKI TOJO, *Japan's leader* • FRANKLIN D. ROOSEVELT, *U.S. President*

HARRY HOPKINS, *presidential aide* • *SAILOR

LIEUTENANT WILLIAM OUTERBRIDGE, *skipper of the U.S.S.* Ward

CAPTAIN JOHN B. EARLE, *a navy Chief of Staff* • PRIVATE GEORGE ELLIOTT, *U.S. Army*

PRIVATE JOSEPH LOCKHARDT, *U.S. Army* • LIEUTENANT KERMIT TYLER, *U.S. Army*

*BUDDY JONES, *age 12* • *LOUIS JONES, *navy dockyard worker*

ADMIRAL CHUICHI NAGUMO, *Japanese navy* • COMMANDER MITSUO FUCHIDA, *Japanese pilot*

*BOB, *U.S. sailor on the U.S.S.* Oklahoma • *HENRY, *U.S. sailor on the U.S.S.* Oklahoma

*MACK, U.S. *sailor on the U.S.S.* Oklahoma • *LOUDSPEAKER

CAPTAIN MERVYN BENNION, *skipper of the U.S.S.* West Virginia

DORIS MILLER, *navy seaman and mess attendant, U.S.S.* West Virginia

ENSIGN VICTOR DELANO *of the U.S.S.* West Virginia

*MRS. EVELYN JONES, *Buddy's mother* • DANIEL INOUYE, *age 17, Hawaiian resident*

MR. INOUYE, *his father* • MRS. INOUYE, *his mother*

JUAN DE CASTRO, *navy dockyard worker* • NARRATORS 1–3

*denotes fictional characters

SCENE 1

NARRATOR 1: In late November 1941, Japan's ambassador, Kichisaburo Nomura, meets with U.S. Secretary of State Cordell Hull.

CORDELL HULL: This is outrageous. Japan has now invaded Thailand, China, and French Indochina. This must stop.

KICHISABURO NOMURA: Why? Western powers like Britain and France have invaded and colonized countries all over Asia. Why can't Japan?

CORDELL HULL: Don't be surprised if President Roosevelt puts an embargo on selling oil and gas to Japan. If you can't get gas, how can you move your armies across Asia?

KICHISABURO NOMURA: You wouldn't dare!

CORDELL HULL: Try us.

NARRATOR 1: Nomura speaks to Japan's leader, General Hideki Tojo.

KICHISABURO NOMURA: The Americans won't budge!

HIDEKI TOJO: If they keep us from getting oil, they will strangle us.

KICHISABURO NOMURA: The United States is much larger and more powerful than Japan.

HIDEKI TOJO: We must remind them that they will pay a price if they attack our interests.

NARRATOR 1: On November 27, General Tojo orders a fleet of ships, including six aircraft carriers, on a secret mission to Hawaii. On December 6, the Japanese embassy in Washington, D.C., begins receiving an urgent fourteen-part message in a secret code.
What they don't know is that the United States has cracked the code, and is receiving the message at the same time. At around 9:30 P.M., thirteen of the fourteen parts of the message are brought to President Franklin D. Roosevelt and an advisor.

FRANKLIN D. ROOSEVELT: It looks as if the Japanese mean war.

HARRY HOPKINS: Since it would be at the convenience of the Japanese, it's too bad that we could not strike the first blow, and prevent any sort of surprise.

FRANKLIN D. ROOSEVELT: No, we can't attack another country first. We are a democracy and a peaceful people. We have a good record.

NARRATOR 1: The fourteenth part of the message doesn't arrive until the next day. General George Marshall sends a telegram to warn American bases along the West Coast, as well as in the Philippines, Panama, and Hawaii. But it will not reach Hawaii until much later.

SCENE 2

NARRATOR 2: Shortly after 5:00 A.M. Sunday morning, December 7, two U.S. ships, the *Condor* and the *Ward,* travel close to each other near Pearl Harbor, Hawaii. Aboard the *Ward,* there is news from the *Condor.*

SAILOR: Skipper, we just received a message from the *Condor*. They say they're seeing a strange white wave. It might be a submarine.

WILLIAM OUTERBRIDGE: Let's keep our eyes on it.

NARRATOR 2: He and his men keep a lookout for the next few hours. At 7:03 A.M. they fire a torpedo. Oil bubbles up and spreads over the water. Later they will learn that they had hit a tiny two-man Japanese submarine, and fired the first shots of United States involvement in World War II. Now, Outerbridge alerts headquarters.

WILLIAM OUTERBRIDGE: I believe we have just attacked a Japanese submarine.

NARRATOR 2: The message goes up the chain of command.

JOHN B. EARLE: It could just be a whale. There have been a lot of false sightings lately. We'll await confirmation before we pass on the warning.

NARRATOR 2: At 7:02 A.M. two U.S. Army privates are at the Army's Opana Radar Station on the northern tip of Oahu. They notice something strange on their radar system.

GEORGE ELLIOTT: Look at that blip. What is it? I've never seen one that big.

JOSEPH LOCKHARDT: Maybe this stupid machine is broken. Let me look. Okay, I'll call the information center. *(He calls.)* Sir? There's a large number of planes coming in from the north, three degrees east.

KERMIT TYLER: There are supposed to be a lot of B-17s flying in from California. They're headed here on their way to the Philippines. Don't worry about it.

GEORGE ELLIOTT: If you're sure, sir.

SCENE 3

NARRATOR 3: At 7:40 A.M. twelve-year-old Buddy Jones and his father, Louis, a navy dockyard worker, are fishing from a dock at Pearl Harbor. From where they are sitting, they can see Battleship Row, where battleships are docked, across the water.

BUDDY JONES: Can you put the worm on my hook, Dad?

LOUIS JONES: Are you scared of a little worm?

BUDDY JONES: I like fishing. I just don't like worming.

LOUIS JONES: Oh, okay, I'll do it.

BUDDY JONES: Dad, can you tell me again which ship is which?

LOUIS JONES: Sure, Buddy. That's Battleship Row, right? You see the ships are in rows. In front is the *Nevada*. Behind it are the *Arizona* and the *Vestal*. Next are the *Tennessee* and the *West Virginia*. Behind them are the *Maryland* and the *Oklahoma*. That little ship behind them is the *Neosha*.

BUDDY JONES: Which ones do you work on, Dad?

LOUIS JONES: Oh, all of them.

BUDDY JONES: Where are the gigantic airplane carriers?

LOUIS JONES: They're out at sea right now.

NARRATOR 3: They hear engines overhead and look up.

BUDDY JONES: Look at those planes, Dad. They have a red circle on the wings.

LOUIS JONES: These drills get more realistic all the time. It looks as if they're dropping fake torpedoes.

SCENE 4

NARRATOR 1: Earlier that morning, at 5:30 A.M., Japanese pilots prepare for their mission on the Japanese airplane carrier *Akagi*, several hundred miles north of Oahu.

CHUICHI NAGUMO: Commander Fuchida, I want you to lead the attack. As Admiral Yamamoto says, "The moment has arrived. The rise or fall of our empire is at stake."

MITSUO FUCHIDA: I am ready, sir.

NARRATOR 1: At 6:00 A.M., one hundred eighty-three Japanese fighters, dive bombers, and torpedo planes take off. Around 7:30 A.M., the clouds break. Fuchida sees Oahu.

MITSUO FUCHIDA: See the way the sun shines through the clouds? It looks just like the Rising Sun on our flag. It's a good omen. *(They narrow in on their target.)* There they are. All eight battleships. Okay, radioman, notify all planes to launch attack.

NARRATOR 1: Just before they attack at 8:00 A.M., the radioman sends the signal to the carriers that their mission will be successful: "Tora . . . Tora . . . Tora."

SCENE 5

NARRATOR 2: At 7:45 A.M., sailors talk aboard the U.S.S. *Oklahoma*.

BOB: I'm going to church. Anybody want to come?

HENRY: Nah. I'm going swimming at Waikiki Beach.

MACK: I'm busy writing my kid sister. It's her birthday.

HENRY: Well, ain't that sweet.

MACK: It's just . . . she's twelve years old and I'm missing her.

HENRY: Here we are in paradise, and Mack is homesick again.

MACK: Hawaii's beautiful, but it sure is far from my family in Kentucky.

HENRY: I do *not* miss Minnesota in December. When I get out of the navy, I'm moving here!

BOB: Well, see you later, guys.

NARRATOR 2: Bob leaves the boat. A few minutes later, Henry and Mack hear an announcement.

LOUDSPEAKER: Man your battle stations! Man your battle stations!

MACK: That's strange. We don't usually have drills on Sunday.

LOUDSPEAKER: Man your battle stations *now*! This is real! Japanese planes are attacking us!

NARRATOR 2: *Boom!* A torpedo hits the side of the *Oklahoma*. Henry and Mack fall down.

HENRY: Oh no. Oh no. It's real.

NARRATOR 2: A second torpedo puts out the ship's lights.

MACK: Wait, it's dark in here. Can you find a flashlight?

HENRY: I'm feeling around . . . here's one . . .

NARRATOR 2: *Boom!* A third torpedo strikes the ship.

HENRY: We have to get on deck, find our battle stations. Let's find a ladder.

NARRATOR 2: *Boom!* A fourth torpedo hits the *Oklahoma*.

MACK: We're going to have to go up the ladder. Hurry! Hurry!

HENRY: Wait, I dropped the flashlight.

NARRATOR 2: He feels around to retrieve it. Boom! A fifth torpedo slams into the ship. This time, Mack and Henry feel the ship spinning.

HENRY: Mack! Mack! Are you okay?

MACK: I bumped my head. What's going on?

HENRY: I found the flashlight. But why are there floor tiles on the ceiling?

MACK: Water's coming in, Henry. Tighten the hatch!

HENRY: I think I've got it watertight. But what do we do now?

NARRATOR 2: Bob is on the land, watching in horror.

BOB: Look at the *Oklahoma!* She's turning over. She's bottom up. Oh, no!

NARRATOR 2: Meanwhile, Mack and Henry are trapped in the *Oklahoma*.

HENRY: I think the ship turned upside down.

MACK: Now what?

Read-Aloud Plays: World War II • Scholastic Teaching Resources

HENRY: We'll just have to sit tight until someone comes to rescue us.

MACK: Sure. They'll find us, won't they?

HENRY: I wish you'd had a chance to mail that letter.

MACK: I wish you'd had a chance to go swimming. *(Water trickles in through an air vent.)* Now what?

HENRY: Take that mattress. Stuff it into the hole.

MACK: Okay, that works, for now. So, do you think we'll drown or suffocate first?

HENRY: Let's not even think about that.

SCENE 6

NARRATOR 3: Captain Mervyn Bennion watches the attack from the deck of the *West Virginia*.

MERVYN BENNION: This is certainly in keeping with Japan's history of surprise attacks.

NARRATOR 3: The deck is hit by bombs and shrapnel. It catches on fire.

MERVYN BENNION: I've been hit!

NARRATOR 3: A young African-American mess attendant, Doris Miller, carries him to safety.

DORIS MILLER: Come on, Captain. You can make it. Captain? Captain?

NARRATOR 3: Captain Bennion dies. An officer, Victor Delano, barks out orders.

VICTOR DELANO: Man the guns, sailors! And you, mess attendant, hand them ammunition.

NARRATOR 3: Like many other African Americans in the Navy, Miller is treated more as a servant than sailor. He is not trained to shoot the big machine guns on deck. But a few minutes later, one of the gunners has fallen. He mans the machine gun, and starts shooting at the planes.

DORIS MILLER: Take that! And that!

NARRATOR 3: But at 8:50 A.M., the damaged ship is sinking

VICTOR DELANO: Abandon ship, men! Abandon ship!

NARRATOR 3: Sailors dive in and try to swim for shore as the *West Virginia* sinks.

SCENE 7

NARRATOR 1: Buddy Jones's mother drives to the dock.

EVELYN JONES: Buddy! Louis! Get in the car!

LOUIS JONES: Thank God you're here. I have to get to the navy base, fast.

EVELYN JONES: I know. Hang on.

NARRATOR 1: When they're nearly there, they get caught in a traffic jam of cars trying to get to Pearl Harbor. More Japanese planes surge overhead. Suddenly, one strafes the road in front of them, narrowly missing their car.

BUDDY JONES: Holy cow!

LOUIS JONES: We're sitting ducks here in the road. I'll run the rest of the way. You guys, hide in the sugar cane fields.

EVELYN JONES: Are you sure?

LOUIS JONES: I'm very sure. Just . . . be safe.

EVELYN JONES: You too, sweetheart.

NARRATOR 1: She pulls the car over to the side of the road, and she and Buddy run into the fields, as bombs explode around them and Japanese planes buzz overhead. Scared, they put their hands over their ears, their heads between knees.

EVELYN JONES: I can't look. Hear that plane? Tell me, Buddy, is it American?

BUDDY JONES: No.

EVELYN JONES: How about that one?

BUDDY JONES: No. None of them are, Mom. None of them.

SCENE 8

NARRATOR 2: Oil from sinking ships leaks into the water of Pearl Harbor. Then, the oil catches on fire. Bullets and bombs explode all around. The U.S.S. *Arizona* has taken a direct hit. More than a thousand men are killed instantly. Hundreds of men from the ships are wounded. Some are hit by gunfire or bombs. Others are burned by oil fires. Hospitals and clinics are soon filled. Injured men are dragged off to places like tennis courts and fields for treatment. Seventeen-year-old Daniel Inouye hears on the radio that Oahu has been bombed.

DANIEL INOUYE: Papa! Did you hear the news? It must be a mistake!

MR. INOUYE: Come outside! See those Japanese planes flying by, and that smoke rising? (*He screams at the sky.*) You fools!

NARRATOR 2: The phone rings. It is the secretary from the Red Cross, calling for volunteers.

DANIEL INOUYE: I'm on my way.

MRS. INOUYE: Where are you going? They'll kill you.

MR. INOUYE: Let him go. He must go.

Read-Aloud Plays: World War II • Scholastic Teaching Resources

NARRATOR 2: Daniel is so busy caring for the wounded, he doesn't go home for five days.

SCENE 9

NARRATOR 3: Meanwhile, the Japanese planes return to their ships.

CHUICHI NAGUMO: What was it was like?

MITSUO FUCHIDA: Four battleships definitely sunk. One sank instantly, another capsized, the other two settled to the bottom of the bay.

CHUICHI NAGUMO: What about the airfields?

MITSUO FUCHIDA: We have achieved a great amount of destruction, but there are still many targets remaining. I recommend we attack again.

CHUICHI NAGUMO: No, I think we have done enough damage for one day.

MITSUO FUCHIDA: But sir . . .

CHUICHI NAGUMO: They won't soon forget what Japan has done.

NARRATOR 3: The ships turn back towards Japan.

SCENE 10

NARRATOR 1: It has been almost a day since the *Oklahoma* was hit. The air is becoming stale, and Henry and Mack are growing weaker. Water has slowly seeped up to their knees.

MACK: If it gets much higher, I don't know what to do. I can't swim.

HENRY: You can't swim and you joined the navy? Well, that figures.

MACK: It doesn't matter anyway. We're going to die here.

HENRY: Don't talk like that, Mack! Your family in Kentucky needs you. Don't give up now. Here, hand me that wrench again. I'm going to try tapping again. S-O-S!

NARRATOR 1: Meanwhile, on top of the upside down *Oklahoma,* navy yard workers listen closely.

LOUIS JONES: You hear that? There's tapping from inside there. But I don't know where it's coming from. It's echoing too much.

JUAN DE CASTRO: We'll have to guess.

NARRATOR 1: Louis and Juan use drills to cut a hole in the ship's hull.

HENRY: Hurry, hurry, hurry! Help us! The compartment's filling with water.

JUAN DE CASTRO: We see you! *(to Louis)* We must work fast. When we make the holes, it changes the air pressure. Trapped air rushes out and the water level rises.

MACK: The water's up to my chest!

JUAN DE CASTRO: Keep calm, young man. We'll get you out.

NARRATOR 2: Jones and de Castro widen the hole with sledgehammers.

HENRY: It's up to my shoulders!

LOUIS JONES: Give me your hands.

NARRATOR 2: He pulls Henry and then Mack out through the hole. Next door, on the ship *Maryland*, thousands of men are waving, clapping, and cheering—including Bob.

BOB (*calling out to them*)**:** Hey, I told you guys you should have gone to church with me!

NARRATOR 2: Henry and Mack wave back and grin. They are thrilled to be rescued. But as they look around, they are horrified by the sight of smoldering ships.

MACK: It looks like the end of the world, Henry.

HENRY: I know, Mack. It looks as if we lost the war.

NARRATOR 3: The mood is grave in Washington, D.C. On December 8, 1941, at 12:29 P.M., President Roosevelt speaks to the United States Congress.

FRANKLIN D. ROOSEVELT: Yesterday, December 7, 1941—a date which will live in infamy —the United States of America was suddenly and deliberately attacked by naval and air forces of the Empire of Japan. . . We will not only defend ourselves to the uttermost, but will make very certain that this form of treachery shall never endanger us again . . . With confidence in our armed forces—with the unbounded determination of our people—we will gain the inevitable triumph—so help us God. I ask that the Congress declare that since the unprovoked and dastardly attack by Japan on Sunday, December 7, a state of war has existed between the United States and the Japanese empire.

NARRATOR 3: Congress quickly agrees with the President. Now the United States officially entered World War II.

EPILOGUE

NARRATOR 3: Pearl Harbor will be Japan's biggest success in World War II. The attack leaves two thousand four hundred three people dead and one thousand one hundred seventy-eight wounded. Eighteen ships are sunk or seriously damaged. Hundreds of planes were damaged or destroyed. The Japanese, on the other hand, lose only five two-man submarines and twenty-nine planes. But though they inflict much damage, within a year six of the eight battleships they attack are fixed and put back into use. And though many Americans had earlier opposed the war, they unite behind the President after Pearl Harbor. From that day on, they fight fiercely to defeat Japan. In the end, as Admiral Yamamoto said, "I am afraid that we have awakened a sleeping tiger and filled him with terrible resolve."

Read-Aloud Plays: World War II • Scholastic Teaching Resources

Background on the Attack of Pearl Harbor

A Nation Changed: For most of its history, Japan lived in isolation from its neighbors. But Japan's leaders in the 1930s had a new vision of Japan. They saw that European nations like France and England had made colonies of huge parts of Asia. Britain controlled British Malaya, rich in rubber and tin. France also controlled French Indochina (what is now Vietnam) with its rich agricultural land. The Dutch controlled Indonesia, rich in oil and gas. Japan was overpopulated. It had few natural resources. Japan decided that it, too, wanted to have colonies. Japan began taking over parts of Asia in 1937, when it attacked China. Next, it invaded Thailand and Southern Indochina. When World War II started, and France, Britain, and other countries were busy fighting for their own survival, Japan saw this as a perfect time to take over these European colonies as well.

Why Pearl Harbor?: Why did the Japanese launch a surprise attack on the United States, when they knew that the United States was a much richer and larger nation than they were? One reason was that America's greatest concentration of naval power was located in Pearl Harbor, Hawaii. If the Japanese knocked out the ships at Pearl Harbor, they could swiftly invade the Philippines and Malaya without fear of reprisal. If Japan could get the oil resources quickly, it might be able to gain even more power. Most experts believe that the Japanese did not expect that they would need to defeat the entire United States forces—they believed that the attack on Pearl Harbor would discourage the United States from wanting to fight and keep it out of the war. Instead, the attack on Pearl Harbor aroused America's fury. Before the war started, a huge number of Americans were isolationists, and did not want to get involved in foreign wars. That all changed after December 7, 1941, the day that, indeed, continues to live in infamy.

CRITICAL THINKING

★ Defeat
Pearl Harbor was a great defeat for the United States. Ask students: *What's the worst defeat you've experienced?* Have them write about what happened. How did they feel, and what did they do about it? What were some of the emotions that went with the experience—betrayal, humiliation, and so forth?

★ Surprise Attack!
Many Americans were outraged that the attack on Pearl Harbor was a surprise attack. Ask students: *If the same number of people were killed, and the same amount of destruction occurred, but it was not a surprise, would it be just as bad or not? What tactics are legitimate in war?* Have them share their reasoning.

★ Holding On to Hope
A number of sailors were trapped in the hull of the *Oklahoma* for more than a day. Ask: *If you were in their situation, what would you think about to keep your hopes up? What would you think about saying to loved ones?*

ACTIVITIES

★ Where Were *They* When . . . :
For many older Americans, the attack on Pearl Harbor was a life-changing event. Many have strong memories of where they were, what was happening around them,

and what happened as a result of the attack. Have students brainstorm a list of questions. Then have them use the questions to interview senior citizens about their Pearl Harbor moment. Have them share their interviews with the class.

★ Where Were *You* When . . . :
Pearl Harbor marked a generation. What historical events have marked your students? Have them brainstorm about news events that have happened during their lifetimes. What events are they most likely to remember? Have students make a time line of events that have occurred since they were born. Which were the most significant?

★ Broadcasting the News
Hawaiian radio reporters were among the first to spread the news of the attack on Pearl Harbor, even as the attack was happening. Have students do further research on the attack at Pearl Harbor. Then have them gather in teams to create their own radio broadcasts about what happened on December 7, 1941. They can read their broadcasts into an audiotape recorder and play them for the class.

★ Japan Today
How has Japan changed as a nation since the attack on Pearl Harbor? Give students a list of questions, including the following: What kind of government does Japan have now? What is its economy like? What is its military like? What kind of relationship does Japan have with the United States? What kinds of products, from TV shows to cars and food, come to the United States from Japan? Then have students try to find the answers by bringing in newspaper and magazine articles about Japan. Have them read the articles and underline passages that they find important and that answer some of the questions above.

★ Our Country
After the attack on Pearl Harbor, most Americans felt very united. Patriotism surged across the country. The attack made many people think about what they love about their country. What values do students think most Americans share? Have students brainstorm a list of American ideals. Then they can make their own posters illustrating some of these American ideals and put them up around the classroom.

Read-Aloud Plays: World War II • Scholastic Teaching Resources

Manzanar

CHARACTERS

*MR. NOBORU NIKAMURA, *a California farmer*

*DAISY NIKAMURA, *age 12*

*TEDDY NIKAMURA, *age 22*

*HELEN NIKAMURA, *age 19*

*FRANKLIN NIKAMURA, *age 7*

*MRS. MICHIKO NIKAMURA

*NEWS REPORTER

*FBI AGENTS 1–2

*RICKY DEAN, *age 12, Daisy's classmate*

*DANIEL KELLER, *age 12, Daisy's classmate*

*PRINCIPAL VIOLET WILSON

*MRS. ANGELA KELLER, *Daniel's mother*

*MRS. BETTY SMITH, *a neighbor* • *SOLDIERS 1–2

*OLD WOMEN 1–2 • NARRATORS 1–3

*denotes fictional characters

SCENE 1

NARRATOR 1: November 1941, dinnertime at the Nikamuras' California farm.

NOBURO NIKAMURA: So, what did you learn about in school today, Daisy?

DAISY NIKAMURA: We learned about the United States Constitution. Did you know that Americans have *inali-* um, *inalienenable*? rights.

TEDDY NIKAMURA: The word is "inalienable." It means that under the U.S. Constitution U.S. citizens have rights that can't be taken away.

HELEN NIKAMURA: That's fine for us kids. We're all *Niseis*—second generation Japanese Americans. We get our citizenship because we were born here. But it's not fair for *Isseis*, people like Mom and Dad who were born in Japan, who aren't allowed to become citizens.

TEDDY NIKAMURA: It's true that the system isn't perfect. But—

HELEN NIKAMURA: Not perfect! How come Asian immigrants can't become citizens, no matter how long they live here, when Europeans can?

TEDDY NIKAMURA: We just have to prove we're good Americans. It's our job to show how we can fit in so they feel more comfortable with us.

HELEN NIKAMURA: How can we show them when no one will even hire me to work at a drugstore? We can't win! I mean, what made you move here in the first place, Father?

NOBURO NIKAMURA: Well, my headstrong daughter, I knew that when my parents died, my oldest brother would inherit my father's farm. That is the way it was done in Japan. A teacher told me, "Go to America. It's the 'land of opportunity.'"

TEDDY NIKAMURA: And it was, wasn't it?

NOBURO NIKAMURA: Yes, it was, Teddy. Your mother and I have worked hard to build our farm. We rented, first, then we bought the land—

HELEN NIKAMURA: Which you put in Teddy's name because he's a citizen and non-citizens like you aren't allowed to buy land.

NOBURO NIKAMURA: Yes, but look at the huge fields of vegetables we grow. I wake up every day and look out at what we've done on our own and I feel so proud. I feel proud of our children, all Americans, all free. Not as free as they should be, maybe, but things are changing every day. You'll see.

TEDDY NIKAMURA: Anyway, it's better than Japan right now!

NOBURO NIKAMURA: Teddy is right. Japan has changed since I was a boy. They've become aggressive. Taking over China and French Indochina. It's frightening! For hundreds of years, we stayed out of other people's business. But things have changed.

HELEN NIKAMURA: I just feel trapped between two worlds sometimes.

SCENE 2

NARRATOR 2: December 7, 1941.

FRANKLIN NIKAMURA: Mommy, why do we have to have rice balls and salmon for breakfast? Can't we have oatmeal? Mikey Porter eats oatmeal every day.

HELEN NIKAMURA: Mother, Father, listen to this! Japan bombed Pearl Harbor.

MICHIKO NIKAMURA: What? It can't be.

NARRATOR 2: Helen turns up the radio. They listen in horror.

NEWS REPORTER: Earlier this morning, the United States of America was suddenly and deliberately attacked by naval and air forces of the Empire of Japan. There has been great damage at Pearl Harbor and very many lives have been lost.

NOBURO NIKAMURA: Is he sure it wasn't the Germans?

TEDDY NIKAMURA: No, Dad. It wasn't the Germans. It was the Japs.

MICHIKO NIKAMURA: Shame on you! How dare you talk that way about your own people?

TEDDY NIKAMURA: I'm sorry, Mom. But Americans are my people. How could the Japanese attack our country? They killed American soldiers!

NOBURO NIKAMURA: Don't turn your back on your heritage.

TEDDY NIKAMURA: My heritage is American! I know America's not perfect. But I can't talk about that right now. Not when America has just been attacked!

MICHIKO NIKAMURA: This is horrible. I fear we'll get caught in the middle.

NOBURO NIKAMURA: Surely people will understand that we are loyal Americans.

MICHIKO NIKAMURA (*putting things into a box*)**:** I'll tell you what we must do. Late tonight, I want you to dig a hole in the backyard. Then put this box into it and bury it.

HELEN NIKAMURA: Not your beautiful kimono! And father's samurai sword!

MICHIKO NIKAMURA: Either bury them or burn them. It isn't safe to keep them.

SCENE 3

NARRATOR 3: A few months later, on February 19, 1942.

HELEN NIKAMURA: Look what they are writing in the papers, Father! It says that President Roosevelt signed an executive order allowing all Japanese Americans to be put into internment camps! We'll only be able to take what we can carry! And we'll only be given twenty-four hours to sell or store our possessions.

TEDDY NIKAMURA: You mean, they would put American citizens in jail?

NOBURO NIKAMURA: I can't believe it. That must be for other people, for spies. Not for us. We work hard. I pay my taxes.

HELEN NIKAMURA: I'm sorry, Father, but President Roosevelt signed it into law.

NARRATOR 3: There is a knock on the door. It is the FBI. Two agents come in and ransack the Nikamuras' possessions. Franklin starts to cry. Daisy squeezes him to keep him quiet.

FBI AGENT 1: So, Nikamura, why did you plant all those tomatoes going north to south?

NOBURO NIKAMURA: What difference does it make how I plant my tomatoes?

FBI AGENT 2: They're pointing right toward the crop duster airport!

NOBURO NIKAMURA: So?

FBI AGENT 1: You know perfectly well that airport is going to be a training airfield for American pilots, don't you? Don't you?

NOBURO NIKAMURA: What? How could I know such a thing?

FBI AGENT 2: You signal Japanese spies with flashlights, don't you?

NOBURO NIKAMURA: Flashlights? What are you talking about?

FRANKLIN NIKAMURA: Daisy and I were playing outside with flashlights last night, Daddy.

FBI AGENT 1: A likely story. We have good reason to suspect you of spying on the United States, Nikamura. Get your toothbrush. You're coming with us.

MICHIKO NIKAMURA: Where are you taking him?

FBI AGENT 2: That's none of your business. And don't think we're not keeping an eye on you, too. My suggestion? Stay indoors, and don't make any trouble.

SCENE 4

NARRATOR 1: March 1942. Daisy and Franklin are on their way to school.

RICKY DEAN: Hey, Japs! Go back where you came from!

FRANKLIN NIKAMURA: What is he talking about? We were born here.

DANIEL KELLER: Leave them alone! They have nothing to do with Pearl Harbor.

RICKY DEAN: Ooh, looks like Keller's a traitor. Traitor! Traitor!

DANIEL KELLER: Be quiet!

NARRATOR 1: They fight, and Daniel gets a black eye. Daisy gets called into the principal's office.

VIOLET WILSON: I don't think you should come back to school. You're causing problems.

DAISY NIKAMURA: But Ricky started it!

VIOLET WILSON: You can hardly blame him for feeling upset.

DAISY NIKAMURA: It's not my fault!

VIOLET WILSON: You're not too popular here. Your people *did* start a war.

DAISY NIKAMURA: What about the Constitution? What about my inali- . . . my rights as a citizen?

VIOLET WILSON: Do you seriously think that anyone thinks of you or any of your people as citizens? American boys are fighting and dying because of people like you.

DAISY NIKAMURA: But I want my education.

VIOLET WILSON: We'll see about that.

NARRATOR 1: But when she goes home, the news is just as bad.

MICHIKO NIKAMURA: Don't bother going back. They're going to be sending us away any day now. I got word that we should be ready to leave with twenty-four hours' notice.

HELEN NIKAMURA: Should we cooperate and go quietly? Or fight for our rights?

MICHIKO NIKAMURA: It won't make a difference. No one sticks up for us. We don't have a single person in the government who is on our side. Anyway, I registered our whole family, so we'll at least all be sent together. Our family number is 12,999.

NARRATOR 1: The days drag on. Finally, they have some good news.

FRANKLIN NIKAMURA: Mom! It's a letter from Dad!

MICHIKO NIKAMURA (*reading it out loud*)**:** "Dearest Family, I am in a Dangerous Alien Enemy Camp in Missoula, Montana. It is very cold here, not like California! Please do not worry about me, but take care of each other." The next part is blacked out by censors. Then it says, "Harvest the strawberries if you can, and be strong until we see each other again. Remember to honor our family name." I hope they let us wait long enough to harvest the strawberries. If they don't, we'll lose a fortune. But at least he is well.

DAISY NIKAMURA: I wish Father were here.

MICHIKO NIKAMURA: I do too, Daisy.

SCENE 5

NARRATOR 2: In the next weeks, few people come to their farmstand. Among the few who do are the Kellers.

ANGELA KELLER: I am so sorry about what's happening. It feels as if some sort of madness is coming over our country. People are so afraid, and they act with fear and ignorance about anything they see as different.

MICHIKO NIKAMURA: Thank you. It's good to know that there are still a few decent people left.

NARRATOR 2: Finally, the Nikamuras get their orders to go.

HELEN NIKAMURA: And here we are, a month from harvest.

NARRATOR 2: There's a knock at the door. In walks Betty Smith, a neighbor.

BETTY SMITH: Oh, hi, do you have some things to sell? I heard you people were leaving.

MICHIKO NIKAMURA: What did you have in mind?

BETTY SMITH: I can offer you five bucks for this old sewing machine.

MICHIKO NIKAMURA: Five dollars! It's new and it's worth a lot more than that.

BETTY SMITH: That's the highest I can go.

MICHIKO NIKAMURA: I'll throw it in the trash before I give it to you at that price!

BETTY SMITH: Touchy, touchy.

MICHIKO NIKAMURA: Get out. Now. *(Mrs. Smith leaves.)* No one helps us. No one cares. We've been neighbors for all these years, and they just look away.

TEDDY NIKAMURA: I just wish there was a way to prove to them we're good Americans.

HELEN NIKAMURA: If this is how good Americans act, I don't care to prove anything to them.

NARRATOR 2: Later, Daniel Keller's mother comes by.

ANGELA KELLER: If you need somewhere to store some things, we have empty room in our garage.

MICHIKO NIKAMURA: Are you sure? Thank you. Teddy will bring over some things tonight.

NARRATOR 2: The Nikamuras pack their bags.

MICHIKO NIKAMURA: There are still a few decent people left, at least. Meanwhile, you need to pack, Daisy. It could be cold where we're going. You need boots. Coats. Clothes. Practical things. How can I reduce a lifetime into two suitcases?

SCENE 6

NARRATOR 3: Finally, it is leaving day. They meet at a local church.

SOLDIER 1: You need to have your number tags hanging around your neck and your suit-cases. Remember, two suitcases per person only! And stay close to your families.

Read-Aloud Plays: World War II • Scholastic Teaching Resources

DANIEL KELLER *(breathless after running up to the church)*: I brought you some chocolates.

DAISY NIKAMURA *(close to tears)*: Thanks, Daniel.

DANIEL KELLER: I'll miss you.

SOLDIER 1 *(to Daisy)*: All right, move on.

HELEN NIKAMURA: Leave her alone! Shame on you, taking our homes and freedom.

SOLDIER 1: Don't blame us, Ma'am. We're doing it for your own protection.

HELEN NIKAMURA *(disgusted)*: If it's for our protection, then why are your guns pointed at *us*?

NARRATOR 3: Finally, they get on the bus. The windows are covered with black paper.

OLD WOMAN 1: Where are they taking us? Why must we leave our homes?

OLD WOMAN 2: Don't frighten the children. We'll find out soon enough.

HELEN NIKAMURA *(after they arrive)*: Where are we?

SOLDIER 2: It's the Santa Anita Racetrack. They haven't finished building the permanent camps. These are transit camps. Now tell me your name and family number. Then, take these white bags. Fill them with hay. These are your mattresses. When you've finished, go find your barracks.

TEDDY NIKAMURA: Where do we sleep?

SOLDIER 2: In the stable. Don't worry, it's very comfortable.

MICHIKO NIKAMURA *(dragging her suitcase and mattress to the stall)*: Human beings in horses' stalls! They still smell like horse manure. This is unbelievable, a nightmare!

NARRATOR 1: A dinner bell rings. The Nikamuras enter the mess hall.

FRANKLIN NIKAMURA: What IS this? It smells disgusting.

DAISY NIKAMURA: It's hot dogs, sauerkraut, and rice. Yuck!

MICHIKO NIKAMURA: Shh, Daisy.

DAISY NIKAMURA: I can't eat this. I'm going to throw up. The sour juice got into the rice.

FRANKLIN NIKAMURA: Look, dust is blowing on my powdered milk. It's disgusting.

MICHIKO NIKAMURA: Don't talk that way. Just eat the rice.

HELEN NIKAMURA: I wish we had some *yakisoba* noodles with fish balls at home.

MICHIKO NIKAMURA: Or crispy shrimp *tempura*.

TEDDY NIKAMURA: Or some *tonkatsu*, pork cutlet with yummy brown sauce.

FRANKLIN NIKAMURA: Now I'm *really* hungry.

SCENE 7

NARRATOR 1: After a few months, they are moved to a "relocation camp" called Manzanar, in a desolate part of the Californian desert. After several hours on a bus, they arrive and look around the bleak landscape. Wind blows through sagebrush.

MICHIKO NIKAMURA: Does the wind always blow so much dust?

TEDDY NIKAMURA: Let's just go to our cabin.

HELEN NIKAMURA: Look at this drafty, dusty tarpaper shack. This place is disgusting!

DAISY NIKAMURA: The cots are all shoved together. I don't want to sleep next to my brother!

MICHIKO NIKAMURA: We have no choice. As we say in Japanese, *shikatanagai*— it can't be helped.

FRANKLIN NIKAMURA: There's no privacy in the bathroom.

HELEN NIKAMURA: Is this little oil stove supposed to keep us warm? It's freezing in here.

MICHIKO NIKAMURA: Look at the cracks between the wooden boards. Dust can blow right in here. We can't live like this. I'm going to complain.

HELEN NIKAMURA: Don't bother. Nobody cares.

TEDDY NIKAMURA: I'll try to patch up the holes in the wood. That should keep some dust out.

MICHIKO NIKAMURA: Thank you. At least we're together.

SCENE 8

NARRATOR 2: At dinner a few months later.

DAISY NIKAMURA: Pork patties, rice, and canned fruit. The fruit touches the rice. Ick!

MICHIKO NIKAMURA: I understand, but you must eat, Daisy. You've gotten way too thin.

DAISY NIKAMURA: I can tell you what I'm NOT going to eat when we leave this place. No marmalade, no apple butter, no fig bars . . .

HELEN NIKAMURA: No powdered milk, no oatmeal . . .

FRANKLIN NIKAMURA: And NO canned meat!

MICHIKO NIKAMURA (*laughing*)**:** It will be nice to eat something that doesn't come out of a can. But this is what we have for now, *shikatanagai*. By the way, children, I got a job.

HELEN NIKAMURA: A job!

MICHIKO NIKAMURA: I can't sit alone in the cabin worrying about your father and sweeping dust all day. I'm going to work in the mess hall. At least I'll earn $12 a month.

Read-Aloud Plays: World War II • Scholastic Teaching Resources

HELEN NIKAMURA: Don't wear yourself out, Mama. But if you want to work, I guess it makes sense.

TEDDY NIKAMURA: I agree, Mother.

HELEN NIKAMURA: See what we've come to? Our innocent father is in prison, and our mother is working for pennies an hour!

TEDDY NIKAMURA: We know we're innocent. But look, it *was* our people who did this. Our people are committing atrocities in Asia every day. Our people are rampaging through one country after another, invading, stealing, and killing.

HELEN NIKAMURA: What are you going to do? Go tell the guards that Mr. Watanabe looks a little suspicious, or that old Mrs. Tanaka is sending secret messages with a mirror? Talk like that and people will think you're an *inu*, a dirty, spying dog.

TEDDY NIKAMURA: Of course I'm not an *inu*! I'm not going to spy on my neighbors.

DAISY NIKAMURA: I'm not going to stay with you two and argue politics. I have my own friends. I'm going to sit at the kids' table. Ta ta!

TEDDY NIKAMURA: She's getting wilder. She's losing touch with the family.

HELEN NIKAMURA: Yes, we must do something. Poor Daisy. I hear her crying at night. She tries acting tough, but this place is making her crazy. She's hurting inside. Just like all of us. Even you, brother.

TEDDY NIKAMURA: Don't look at me like that, Helen. Don't.

NARRATOR 2: One day, they get a surprise. Father is returned to them. They are joyful at first. But their father has changed.

FRANKLIN NIKAMURA: Why is Father so gloomy all the time? You've gotten used to it, why can't he? You're working hard and he does nothing.

MICHIKO NIKAMURA: Your father is proud. All his life, he has been providing for us. Now he has nothing and feels helpless.

SCENE 9

NARRATOR 3: A few months later, in early 1943, every internee over the age of seventeen is required to fill out a Registration and Loyalty questionnaire. People argue about it for months.

HELEN NIKAMURA: Okay, here are the two toughest questions: "Question 27: Are you willing to serve in the armed forces of the United States on combat duty, wherever "ordered?"

MICHIKO NIKAMURA: If Teddy answers yes, is he automatically signing up for the army?

HELEN NIKAMURA: I don't know! And listen to this. "Question 28: Will you swear unqualified allegiance to the United States of America and faithfully defend the United States from any or all attack by foreign or domestic forces, and forswear any form of allegiance or obedience to the Japanese emperor, or any other foreign government, power or organization?"

MICHIKO NIKAMURA: We aren't allowed to be American citizens, but they want us to give up our Japanese citizenship? That means your father and I won't be citizens of any country. That's frightening.

HELEN NIKAMURA: And for us *Nisseis*, that question is a complete insult. We were born and brought up here. Of course we have no loyalty to the Japanese emperor. Some people are answering "No" to those questions.

NOBURO NIKAMURA: But I hear they're putting them in jail for disloyalty.

HELEN NIKAMURA: We're already in jail.

TEDDY NIKAMURA: I'm signing yes to both. If I get sent to the army, fine.

HELEN NIKAMURA: I'm signing yes to both too. But I'm appalled they would even ask.

NARRATOR 3: One day, Franklin decides to help his father.

FRANKLIN NIKAMURA: Look, Daddy, they gave us grass seeds.

NOBURO NIKAMURA: I don't care.

FRANKLIN NIKAMURA: Okay! I'll do it. I should throw the seeds in front of the cabin, and wait for rain?

NOBURO NIKAMURA: No! I didn't spend my life as a farmer for my son to think that's how you grow things! I'd better help you.

NARRATOR 3: Within a few months, the Nikamuras have a carefully tended garden, and Mr. Nikamura has joined a gardening club.

SCENE 10

NARRATOR 1: In 1944, Teddy joins the All-Japanese 442nd Infantry.

HELEN NIKAMURA: I can't believe you're going into the army.

TEDDY NIKAMURA: It makes me mad that they make us fight in a segregated unit. But I guess it's good in a way, because we'll all watch each other's backs.

DAISY NIKAMURA: What if something bad happens to you?

TEDDY NIKAMURA: I want to prove myself, Daisy. I can't stand being here. Maybe if we prove ourselves, they won't make you and Mom and Dad live here like caged animals.

NARRATOR 1: He leaves. A few months later . . .

DAISY NIKAMURA: What are you doing?

HELEN NIKAMURA: I'm filling out a form for the War Relocation Agency Leave Clearance program. I've applied for a job at a hotel fixing salads at a restaurant.

DAISY NIKAMURA: You're deserting me!

HELEN NIKAMURA: I need to make some money to help us when the war ends.

DAISY NIKAMURA: Helen, are you sure you should leave the family?

HELEN NIKAMURA: I'm going to need your help. You're going to have to be the big one now. Help Franklin. He's getting wild. We can't help being put in prison for what we didn't do. But we can help how we take care of each other.

DAISY NIKAMURA: That's not fair!

HELEN NIKAMURA: You're right. It's very unfair. I wish life were a lot fairer for you.

NARRATOR 1: A few months later, Helen leaves for Chicago. She writes a letter home.

HELEN NIKAMURA: Dear Mom and Dad. I miss you. People stare at me. We stopped at a hamburger joint on the bus here, and one guy said, "I don't serve Japs." It really hurt. Sometimes I pretend to be Chinese, just so people will leave me alone. Still, I'm earning money, and I'm saving it for when we get out.

NARRATOR 1: One evening at the camp the family lines up in the mess hall.

MICHIKO NIKAMURA: Our poor children, Helen in Chicago, and Teddy off in Italy. They're so far away. At least we have Daisy and Franklin with us.

NOBURO NIKAMURA: What a way for them to grow up. Look at them over there.

FRANKLIN NIKAMURA: I'm going to sit with my friends, not with Mom and Dad.

DAISY NIKAMURA: It's up to us to help them feel as if we still have a family.

FRANKLIN NIKAMURA: But it's so boring! It's more fun to be with my friends.

DAISY NIKAMURA: I know, we're growing up in a weird way, but *shikatanagai*—it can't be helped. We have to pull together now, for all our sakes. Okay?

FRANKLIN NIKAMURA: Okay, okay, Sis. If you put it that way, I'll try.

EPILOGUE

NARRATOR 2: After the war ended, many Japanese Americans were broke, having lost their homes and businesses. Many had broken spirits as well. Finally the Civil Liberties Act of 1988 was passed into law. This act authorized the government to pay survivors of the camps twenty thousand dollars each—and to apologize for the wrongs done to them.

Background on the Internment of Japanese Americans

A Present Danger?: After the Japanese attacks on America, life in the United States changed for Americans of Japanese descent. At that time, the majority of Japanese living in the United States lived on the West Coast. But President Franklin D. Roosevelt decided that Japanese—potential traitors in his eyes—living along the coast closest to Japan put the United States in too much danger. In February 1942 he signed Executive Order 9066. This designated certain areas within the United States as having high military sensitivity, and allowed that anyone deemed threatening could be evacuated from these areas. Because the West Coast states were designated as military zones, the groundwork was laid for evacuating the Japanese from their homes. Roosevelt declared that all Japanese-American men, women, and children on the West Coast should be imprisoned. Most were held in ten large internment camps located in desolate spots in California, Wyoming, Idaho, Utah, Colorado, and Arkansas. Some wound up in smaller camps scattered around the United States.

A History of Prejudice: Because of anti-Asian prejudice, most Asians born outside of the United States were not allowed to immigrate or become American citizens after 1924. That changed for those from China, the Philippines, and India during the 1940s—these nations were wartime allies of the United States. But it wouldn't be until 1952 that Japanese would be able to immigrate. Not until that year would Japanese-born residents of the United States be allowed citizenship, either. Despite these unfair laws, and a number of others—including restrictions against marrying a white person and owning their own property—tens of thousands of Japanese immigrants made good lives for themselves in the United States.

Leaving the Camps: The camps didn't close until 1946. But during the war, the U.S. government allowed some Japanese to leave the camps for several reasons. Some were allowed to leave the camps temporarily to help harvest sugar beets in the American West. Others, like Helen in the play, were allowed to leave the camps to find work or attend college in the East or Midwest on a special work release program. Those who left under this program had to be sponsored. Most of those allowed to leave were between the ages of fourteen and thirty-five. Though they were free, many of them experienced prejudice, and felt guilty and worried about those family members who remained trapped in camp.

Japanese-American Soldiers: Others, like Teddy, left to fight in the U.S. military. The all-Japanese-American 442nd Infantry had an extremely distinguished record during the war. They fought so bravely and fiercely that they won more than eighteen thousand individual medals, including the Congressional Medal of Honor.

CRITICAL THINKING

★ Coping
Many people coped with their imprisonment in Manzanar and other camps by taking classes, planting gardens, and starting hobbies. Ask students: *What special skills or interests would you share if you were in their situation? What would you want to learn? Why could learning new skills help people to cope?*

★ Family Life
Many people at Manzanar said that the experience of living there destroyed the closeness of family life. Ask: *What kinds of experiences keep families feeling stable and close? What, specifically, about life in Manzanar might have undermined that?*

Read-Aloud Plays: World War II • Scholastic Teaching Resources

★ Speaking Up

In the 1940s only a small number of people, like the Kellers in the play, were willing to speak up and help their Japanese-American neighbors. In school, Daniel Keller faced a beating and suspension for standing up for Daisy Nikamura. Ask: *Have you ever stood up for someone who was being picked on or teased? What happened? Would you do it again? Why or why not?*

ACTIVITIES

★ Civil Liberties

In 1988 the United States government apologized to Japanese Americans for imprisoning them without proof of any wrongdoing. Read the United States Constitution and Bill of Rights to learn what rights are guaranteed to citizens. Have students brainstorm and make a list of their rights. How do people keep these civil rights? One way is to become educated about them. Another way is to help organizations that support freedom of speech and human rights, such as the American Civil Liberties Union. To learn more about how you can get involved, contact the ACLU at: http://www.aclu.org, or write to American Civil Liberties Union, 125 Broad Street, 18th Floor, New York, NY 10004.

★ Packing List

In this play, Michiko Nikamura has a hard time deciding which of her possessions to pack up into her allotment of two suitcases. If you had to pack up your possessions into two suitcases like the Nikamuras did, what would you take with you? (Remember to consider the climate.) What would you most regret leaving? Make a packing list of the top ten items you would pack up in your suitcase.

★ Defending Yourself

Just like the Nikamura children in the play, many Japanese Americans were divided about how much they should oppose their imprisonment. Some feared that if they protested, they would seem less sympathetic and more threatening. Have students try pretending to be Japanese Americans in early 1942. Have them write letters to the editor of a local newspaper making a case for why they should not be put into internment camps.

★ Flavor of Japan

One of the things the characters in the play most missed was being able to make the foods of their land of origin. Help students to learn more about what they were missing by giving them a taste of one of the world's greatest cuisines. In many stores you can purchase appetizers such as California roll *sushi, gyoza* (dumplings), and *edamame* (steamed soy beans), and other delicious treats. It is also very simple to prepare ramen noodles. After giving students a taste, ask them what special foods come out of their own cultural traditions. Would they miss them if they couldn't have them? *Note: Please check if students have any related food allergies prior to using this activity.*

★ Voting

One problem the Nikamuras and thousands of other Japanese-American immigrants had was that they lacked a voice in the government because they couldn't vote. Talk to students about how many citizens don't take advantage of that precious right and responsibility. Have students brainstorm ways to get more Americans to vote. Three ideas: Have students make bookmarks urging people to vote and give them to a local library to distribute to patrons. Have students make pro-voting posters and put them up around town. Or ask local grocery stores if they can have plain grocery bags to decorate with pro-voting messages. Then they can return the decorated bags to the store for customers to use.

Operation Overlord:
The D-Day Story

CHARACTERS

*JACK, *a U.S. army soldier* • *ERNIE, *a U.S. army soldier*

FIELD MARSHAL GERD VON RUNDSTEDT, *a German general*

FIELD MARSHAL ERWIN ROMMEL, *a German general*

CAPTAIN HELMUTH LANG, *a German, aide to Rommel*

GENERAL DWIGHT D. EISENHOWER, *head of the Allied forces*

MAJOR GENERAL WALTER BEDELL SMITH, *an American officer*

CAPTAIN J.N. STAGG, *Royal Air Force meteorologist*

ADMIRAL SIR BERTRAM RAMSAY, *a British officer*

AIR CHIEF MARSHAL SIR ARTHUR W. TEDDER, *a British officer*

AIR CHIEF MARSHAL SIR TRAFFORD LEIGH-MALLORY, *a British officer*

GENERAL BERNARD MONTGOMERY, *a British officer*

PRIVATE JOHN STEELE, *U.S. paratrooper* • *CORPORAL BILL • *SOLDIER

*NAVY SEAMAN • *MEDIC • OBERST BODO ZIMMERMAN, *a German officer*

MAJOR GENERAL HORST VON BUTTLAR-BRANDENFELS, *a German officer*

MAJOR GENERAL DOCTOR HANS SPEIDEL, *a German officer*

NARRATORS 1–3

* denotes fictional characters.

Read-Aloud Plays: World War II • Scholastic Teaching Resources

SCENE 1

NARRATOR 1: June 3, 1944. Two soldiers shiver under a dripping tarp. They are eating their supper off metal trays in a U.S. Army base in southern England.

JACK: I'm beginning to wonder if this so-called battle is ever going to happen. Instead, here we sit in England waiting around and doing battle exercises in the rain.

ERNIE: At least we got to see Big Ben.

JACK: When will we get to Paris and see the Eiffel Tower?

ERNIE: Well, I did hear they have four hundred different kinds of cheese in France. But seriously, Jack, aren't you scared? We've never been in a battle before.

JACK: I *was* scared. Now, I'm bored. We came here to do a job. Now I just want to do it. The sooner we get it over with, the sooner we go home. Why, are you feeling scared? Are you afraid you're going to be killed?

ERNIE: No. I mean, yes. But that's not all I'm afraid of. I signed up to protect my country and to make my parents proud. But I hate the sight of blood. What if I'm a coward?

JACK: I'm sure you'll be fine. All this waiting around is making everybody feel crazy.

ERNIE: I wish I was like you, Jack. You aren't scared of anything.

JACK: Sure I am.

ERNIE: Like what?

JACK: Like trying four hundred kinds of cheese.

ERNIE: Very funny.

JACK: Oh, come on, pal. We can do it. We'll stick together, okay?

SCENE 2

NARRATOR 2: June 4. Two German generals meet in their headquarters near the coast of France.

GERD VON RUNDSTEDT: Rommel, tell me. What is happening on the Atlantic front?

ERWIN ROMMEL: We've been preparing defenses all along the French coast for years. We've put millions of mines in the water and on the beach, and built huge concrete fortifications. And yet, I still worry we won't be prepared when the Allies come.

GERD VON RUNDSTEDT: My dear Rommel, don't worry so much about stopping the Allies on the beach. If they come inland, we can surround them before an invasion goes any farther.

ERWIN ROMMEL: Sir, I respectfully disagree. I believe we need to get them on the beach before they can establish themselves inland.

GERD VON RUNDSTEDT: Very well, Rommel. I am happy to have you prepare for the invasion. I'm sure it will come. But where, I wonder.

ERWIN ROMMEL: The place that makes sense is the Pas de Calais. It's the point where the British channel is closest to German-controlled France. Besides, the Allies keep bombing it, so that must be the place. But you never know where an enemy will strike. Everything must be in a state of perfect readiness when they come, if they come.

GERD VON RUNDSTEDT: Thank you, Rommel. I know how hard you've been working. Why don't you take a few days off?

ERWIN ROMMEL: Thank you, sir.

NARRATOR 2: On the drive to Germany, Rommel talks to his aide.

ERWIN ROMMEL: What is the weather report, Lang?

HELMUTH LANG: We should expect high winds and rain, sir.

ERWIN ROMMEL: Now I feel more comfortable leaving the front. The Allies are unlikely to attack in the next few days. Not with this weather. In my experience, the Americans only like to attack when the weather is perfect.

HELMUTH LANG: Yes, sir.

ERWIN ROMMEL: But I worry about our soldiers on the Atlantic front. They're either too old, too young, or they're from captured territories like Poland and Romania. They can hardly be trusted to give their all fighting for the fatherland. We know the Allies will invade. But we must stop them right on the beach, no matter what von Rundstedt says.

SCENE 3

NARRATOR 3: On the evening of June 4, Allied leaders meet at the Supreme Headquarters of the Allied Expeditionary Force (SHAEF) in a small town outside of London, England.

DWIGHT D. EISENHOWER: We've been building up for this invasion for more than a year. We must stop the Nazis in their tracks.

WALTER BEDELL SMITH: Surely the Germans suspect we will attack.

DWIGHT D. EISENHOWER: Yes, but they must not find out when or where. They think we're going to attack at the Pas de Calais, and I want to keep it that way. And hopefully, we'll make our move soon. We've already recalled the troops once. Can we start the invasion tomorrow? You're the Royal Air Force meteorologist, Captain Stagg. What do you say?

J.N. STAGG: As you know, gentlemen, we have had some bad weather in the last day or so. This storm makes our operation impossible. But I'm anticipating a break in the storm, which will continue through the morning of June 6. But then conditions will become bad again. It's very iffy, sirs, but we've got a small window of opportunity.

BERTRAM RAMSAY: We must decide quickly, General Eisenhower. If the operation is to take place on Tuesday morning, I will need to give the order in the next half hour. Otherwise we'll need to refuel, and we won't be ready to fight on the seventh.

WALTER BEDELL SMITH *(to Eisenhower)***:** It's a gamble, sir. We have already planned Operation Overlord to be launched on the fifth, sixth, or seventh of June. We need a full moon so our paratroopers can see their way once they've landed. If we don't attack by the seventh, we won't be able to attack for another month. And then the element of surprise will be lost.

ARTHUR W. TEDDER: I'm worried that if clouds cover the Normandy Coast, the air forces won't be able to see well enough to drop their bombs.

TRAFFORD LEIGH-MALLORY: And if they can't bomb, they won't be able to knock out any German defenses. That will make hard going for our boys.

DWIGHT D. EISENHOWER: What do you say, Monty?

BERNARD MONTGOMERY: I would say, Go.

DWIGHT D. EISENHOWER *(after a long silence)***:** I am quite positive we must give the order. I don't like it, but there it is . . . . I don't see how we can do anything else.

SCENE 4

NARRATOR 1: More than eight hundred American planes carrying thirteen thousand para-troopers fly over the town of Ste.-Mere-Eglise. Their plan is to land a few miles outside of the town, then sweep in and capture it. But heavy winds blow about thirty American soldiers right to the center of town. Among them is Private John Steele. As he drifts down, a bullet hits his foot.

JOHN STEELE: Ouch! Uh-oh!

NARRATOR 1: His parachute catches on the church's steeple, and he dangles from the roof.

JOHN STEELE: Maybe I can cut myself down. Let's see, where's my knife? Here . . . oh no!

NARRATOR 1: He drops it and it clatters onto the street far below. Still trapped on the steeple, he watches helplessly.

JOHN STEELE: Our men are being slaughtered!

NARRATOR 1: Steele sees another American paratrooper, caught in a tree, riddled with machine gun fire. Yet another paratrooper screams as he drifts right into a burning house. For the next two hours, he hangs helplessly above the battle, pretending to be dead. Finally American soldiers win the battle and Germans flee the town at 4:30 A.M. By dawn, the paratroopers have confused the Germans by cutting telephone lines, and kept them from bringing in reinforcements.

SCENE 5

NARRATOR 2: On the night of June 5, Ernie and Jack are aboard a boat on its way to Omaha Beach on the Normandy Coast.

CORPORAL BILL: Men, this is it. The invasion is on. Let me read a message for you from General Eisenhower: "Soldiers, Sailors, and Airmen of the Allied Expeditionary Force! You are about to embark upon the Great Crusade, toward which we have striven these many months. The eyes of liberty-loving people everywhere march with you . . . ."

JACK: Well, isn't that sweet.

ERNIE: Good old Ike.

JACK: Come on, did you ever see anything like this? Look at this fleet of thousands and thousands of ships: destroyers, battleships, Higgins boats, anything that can float. I wish I had a camera. Nothing like this has happened in the whole history of the world.

ERNIE: You're thinking about history. Tomorrow we may *be* history.

JACK: Oh, come on, Ernie. Tomorrow we'll *make* history. We're doing something good, remember? Feel proud.

NARRATOR 2: But as the night wears on, their patience wears thin.

JACK: I've already written to my best girl and my mother. Now, I just want to get it over with.

NARRATOR 2: As the hours pass, more and more of the men get seasick.

ERNIE: I don't even have anything left to throw up.

JACK: What a waste of turkey with all the trimmings.

ERNIE: Don't say that word.

JACK: Turkey? Or trimmings?

ERNIE: Don't talk about it.

NARRATOR 2: He throws up again. Finally, it is 7:00 A.M. The boat approaches the beach. Bullets ping all around them.

Read-Aloud Plays: World War II • Scholastic Teaching Resources

ERNIE: I'm worried that with our heavy equipment, we won't even get ashore. Between our weapons, entrenching tools, first aid kits, gas masks, rations, canteens, and everything else, we must weigh three hundred pounds. How can our life preservers even hold us up?

JACK: Oh, Ernie, we'll be okay, don't worry.

NARRATOR 2: German bombs hit a nearby boat, and it starts to sink. Men fall out of the boat. Dragged down by their heavy equipment, some start drowning.

SOLDIER: Help! Help! I'm drowning.

ERNIE: Hey! Stop! We've got to save that guy.

NAVY SEAMAN: Sorry, guys. Our job is to get you on shore. This isn't a rescue ship.

ERNIE: But—

CORPORAL BILL: Keep your heads down, men. As soon as we're spotted we'll catch enemy fire.

NARRATOR 2: Sickened, Ernie throws up again. A bullet flies right past his head.

JACK: Ernie, your hands are shaking. Calm down.

ERNIE: Look at that beach. It's covered with barbed wire, beach obstacles, and mines! How are we supposed to get there?

NAVY SEAMAN: Okay men, here's where you get out.

ERNIE: But the water's up to our chins.

NAVY SEAMAN: I can't get any closer or I'll hit a mine.

ERNIE: But—

CORPORAL BILL: Go, soldier. That's an order.

JACK: Stick with me, pal. We'll be trying out four hundred kinds of cheese in no time.

ERNIE: I'm scared, Jack.

JACK: One, two, three, JUMP.

NARRATOR 2: The friends jump into the water. Suddenly, Jack screams.

ERNIE: Jack! Are you okay?

JACK: My arm! I've been hit.

(Ernie feels faint as he sees Jack's wound.)

ERNIE (to himself)**:** I was relying on him. But now he needs me. (He speaks to Jack.) Let me help you.

NARRATOR 2: He pulls Jack onto the beach. They face heavy fire. They hide between piles of bodies and washed up equipment. All around them, men are confused. Some start crying.

JACK: Know what? I wish I had a hamburger right now. And an ice cold soda.

ERNIE: Why are you talking like that? We're in the middle of a battle, Jack! Get a hold of yourself. Don't go into shock!

NARRATOR 2: He bandages Jack's arm to try to stop the flow of blood.

JACK: I'm tired. I think I'll take a little nap.

ERNIE: NO!

NARRATOR 2: They hear officers yelling up and down the beach.

CORPORAL BILL: I'm sick of being pinned down. Let's move, men.

JACK: Where's my mother? I want my mama.

ERNIE: We can't stay here.

JACK: Why not?

ERNIE: First, because you're losing too much blood. Second, because we're hiding behind a truck and it's full of gas. Look at those burned tanks over there. If the Germans throw a grenade at it, it will explode and we'll be dead. We have to get under that cliff.

JACK: I can't move. I'm afraid. If we move we'll get killed.

ERNIE: I'm afraid too, buddy. But we have to look for a medic for you. It's your only chance. Just put your good arm over my shoulder, okay? One, two, three, go.

NARRATOR 2: They run for the bottom of the cliff, jumping over bodies and dodging heavy fire.

ERNIE: Medic! Medic! Can you help my friend here?

MEDIC: Sure thing. We'll get him all bandaged up and send him back to England.

ERNIE: Thanks. See you back in England, okay, pal?

JACK: See, Ernie? You're a pretty tough guy when you have to be.

SCENE 6

NARRATOR 3: In the morning, von Rundstedt's aide Bodo Zimmerman talks to General von Buttlar-Brandenfels at Hitler's headquarters.

BODO ZIMMERMAN: When are we going to get those tanks? We need them as soon as possible.

HORST VON BUTTLAR-BRANDENFELS: You had no right to alert these divisions without our approval. You are to halt the *Panzer* tanks immediately. Nothing is to be done before the Fuhrer makes his decision!

BODO ZIMMERMAN: But, sir . . .

HORST VON BUTTLAR-BRANDENFELS: Hitler has taken a sleeping pill and we will *not* wake him.

BODO ZIMMERMAN (*telephoning his boss, General von Rundstedt*)**:** Sir, he said he won't wake the Fuhrer . . .

GERD VON RUNDSTEDT: This is outrageous! Must we lose a war because of that . . . that . . . Bohemian corporal?

NARRATOR 3: At 10:15, General Hans Speidel calls Rommel.

HANS SPEIDEL: I'm sorry we forgot to tell you. There's been an invasion. In Normandy.

ERWIN ROMMEL: In Normandy? You're sure?

HANS SPEIDEL: Of course I'm sure.

ERWIN ROMMEL: How stupid of me. We must hurry back. (*He gets into a car.*) Hurry, driver! They got through the defensive wall. Oh my. I was right all along.

SCENE 7

NARRATOR 1: Back on Omaha Beach . . .

CORPORAL BILL: Now we have to smash that wall, climb that cliff, and get those Germans. We're stuck under here. I didn't come all this way to die under a cliff. The only way to be safe is to move. We can't stay here, paralyzed.

NARRATOR 1: Corporal Bill points to an abandoned bulldozer that is loaded with dynamite for blowing up defensive walls.

CORPORAL BILL: I need a volunteer to drive this thing.

NARRATOR 1: No one moves.

CORPORAL BILL: Aren't any of you brave enough to drive this thing?

ERNIE: Oh, what the heck. I guess this war's got to start somewhere. Sir? I'll do it. (*He gets in the bulldozer.*) This is for Jack. And for all the other Jacks out here fighting and dying.

NARRATOR 1: *Boom!* He smashes through the wall.

CORPORAL BILL: Now, move men. Go! Go!

NARRATOR 1: Ernie and other soldiers pour through the gap he has made. By the end of the day, the soldiers have fought their way off Omaha Beach and are a mile inland.

CORPORAL BILL: Good job, Private.

ERNIE: I never thought we'd make it up the cliff.

CORPORAL BILL: If it weren't for a few brave men like you, we wouldn't have.

ERNIE: Thanks, sir. But everything I learned about bravery I learned from Jack.

CORPORAL BILL: Don't forget what he taught you. You're going to need all the courage you can get before this war is over. We'll win it, for sure. But it won't be easy.

EPILOGUE

NARRATOR 2: By the end of the day, there are two thousand five hundred American soldiers dead, wounded, and missing on Omaha beach alone. Many months of fighting lay ahead for the Allies. Nazi Germany would not surrender until May 1945. But despite its horrendous costs, D-Day was a victory.

Read-Aloud Plays: World War II • Scholastic Teaching Resources

Background on the D-Day Invasion

A Massive Undertaking: The military term *D-Day* refers to any day for which a major battle is scheduled (just as *H-Hour* stands for the exact hour for which the battle is scheduled). But there's only one D-Day that will truly be remembered by that name. That day is June 6, 1944, when more than three million Allied military men from the United States, Britain, Canada, and the occupied countries of mainland Europe took part in one of the most awesome sea invasions ever, an invasion officially named Operation Overlord. These sailors, Air Force fighters, and the Coast Guard crossed the English Channel at one of its widest points to attack the Germans on land they held in Normandy, France. They would land at five beaches, spread out over fifty miles, which they called Omaha, Utah, Gold, Juno, and Sword. It was incredibly difficult, and risky. In the months before the invasion, thousands of planes and jeeps were hidden under camouflage and in the forests. Huge amounts of weapons, food, and transport vehicles were stored in secret in preparation for the invasion. The assault would spearhead the effort to take back France, and the rest of Europe, from the grip of the Nazis. Nothing like this massive invasion over water had ever been tried before. Months in the planning, it would be a disastrous setback for the Allies if it failed.

A Hard Day: D-Day got off to a rocky start, particularly on Omaha Beach. More than 90 percent of the Americans' casualties that day took place there. Things went more smoothly for the Americans who landed on Utah Beach. They also went more easily for the British, Canadian, and Continental troops who landed on Gold, Sword, and Juno beaches, though they too faced harsh enemy fire. All in all, about 10,000 members of the Allies were killed, wounded, or missing by the end of the day. There were somewhere between 4,000 and 9,000 German casualties. But though the costs were high—and many things during D-Day didn't go quite as planned—the Allies succeeded in getting a toehold in France. They would press forward until the Germans finally surrendered on May 8, 1945.

CRITICAL THINKING

★ Facing Fear

In the play Ernie finds he has more courage than he thought he did. Ask students: *Have you ever been in a tough situation in which you feared you would be a failure, but found that you were more capable than you thought?* Have them share situations where that took place. *Is there any other way they would have discovered that ability? What are the benefits of stressful situations? What are the drawbacks?*

★ Sacrifice

Thousands of young American soldiers who crossed the English channel on June 6, 1944, faced one of the most difficult challenges human beings ever confront—going into battle knowing that they could well be killed. Thousands of Americans died for their country on D-Day. Ask: *Would you be willing to die for your country? What causes, if any, would you be willing to sacrifice your life for?* Remind students that people who give up their lives for a cause won't be around to see if their cause succeeded. And yet people have made such sacrifices since the dawn of human history. Ask students why people might make that choice.

★ Deception

Winston Churchill once said, "In wartime, truth is so precious that she should always be attended by a bodyguard of lies." During D-Day, Allied troops fooled the Germans into thinking that they were going to attack at the Pas de Calais instead of in Normandy. Most people would find that kind of trick reasonable. Ask students: *Can you imagine any situations where lying to an enemy during wartime crosses the line? What about other actions? What would* not *be fair to do to an enemy, even during a war?*

ACTIVITIES

★ Honoring a Vet

Call a local veteran's hospital and ask what you can do to help and support veterans. Ideas include writing letters and cards of appreciation, raising money to buy something useful to bring the vets comfort (after finding out what they might need), and going to a hospital to sponsor a party, do a performance, or make a regular series of visits.

★ Leader Wanted

Certain people showed great leadership during D-Day. Ask students: *What qualities are important in a leader?* Have them brainstorm a list of admired leaders, both throughout history and in their own lives. What do these leaders do that they respect? When they are done brainstorming, have students use their list of ideas in making up their own "Leader Wanted" classified ads.

★ D-Day News Report

D-Day could never have been won without the efforts and sacrifices of British, Canadian, and Continental soldiers. Have students research the troops who fought on Gold, Sword, and Juno beaches. Then have students pretend to be news reporters and write an account of some significant actions taken by these Allied soldiers. Share accounts with the class.

★ Remembering Things Differently

Help students to understand the idea of individual perspective in understanding historical events. Help them to understand that many factors can change a person's point of view by asking them the following questions. Ask students: *How do you think different characters in the play would remember D-Day in later years? What would stand out in your memory if you were German as opposed to a member of the Allies? How would it be different if you were a general in London or Berlin, as opposed to a soldier on the battlefield? Would you be pleased or not with the results of D-Day?* Have students write an account of D-Day from the perspective of at least three different characters in the play, such as Field Marshal Rommel, General Eisenhower, and Ernie, an American soldier.

★ Map It!

Ask students to work in groups making large maps of Germany today. Have them put in major cities, rivers, mountain ranges, and other features. Next, ask them to surround the maps with fact cards, photos, and illustrations. Ask them about how life in Germany has changed since D-Day in 1944. Put the finished maps on your bulletin board.